From Jehovah's Witnesses

Revised Edition

Dwight A. Hayes

The cover photo pictures the dungeon, excavated beneath Caiaphas' house in Mount Zion, Jerusalem. The Lord Jesus was likely a prisoner here between trials. Peter may have referred to this very site when he said to Jesus, "Lord, I am ready to go with you to prison and death." (Luke 22:33)

Copyright © 2011 by Dwight A. Hayes

Revised 2017

Cover design by Mary K. Turner

Book design by Michael Abraham

Printed in the USA

All rights reserved.

No portion of this book may be reproduced in any form without the written permission of the publisher, except for brief excerpts in written reviews.

Unless otherwise indicated, all Scripture quotations are from the HOLY BIBLE: NEW INTERNATIONAL VERSION ®, Copyright © 1973, 1978, 1984

by International Bible Society.

Used by permission of Zondervan.

All rights reserved.

Other Scripture quotations are from:

Authorized King James Version (KJV)

The Living Bible (a paraphrase), Tyndale House (LB)

The New American Standard Bible,

Lockman Foundation, (NASB)

Phillips Modern English,

The Macmillan Company, (Phillips)

Revised Standard Version, Licensee,

Zondervan Publishing, (RSV)

The New World Translation of The Holy Scriptures,

Watch Tower Bible & Tract Society, (NWT)

Dedication

To my grandchildren:

Logan

Zachary

Shane

Jacob

Ariana

Grant

Douglas

Elizabeth

Jared

Elijah

Meredith

Cora

Reagan

&

Silas

May you hold firmly to the faith of your grandparents.

Preface

This book is arranged in several sections: first you will find the story of my life. Then I present several important issues where Jehovah's Witnesses teachings differ significantly from historical Christianity.

The Appendix features questions I have been asked over the past thirty-seven years. I attempt to provide practical answers. It is my hope that you, the reader, may reference this section from time-to-time.

During the past six years, since this book was published, new issues have arisen concerning Jehovah's Witnesses. In this revision I have highlighted two new controversies, Watchtower Shunning – Is it Hate Speech? And, What About a Pedophilia Epidemic Among Jehovah's Witnesses? These topics are followed by an Index.

You will discover a recurring Holy Land theme embedded in my account. I am convinced that God's Old Testament promises to Israel are being fulfilled in our time. The Land is being restored, the Jewish people are returning to their homeland, and the nations of the world are turning against Jerusalem (see Zechariah 12:3,9). My interest in the land which God says he loves has drawn me to that region. Experiences which I have recalled from the Holy Land are but a small sample of my encounters there.

I considered placing Scripture references in footnotes; the text might be more readable. But I decided to leave the Bible references in the main text, because I wish to remind you, the reader, that the Bible is my authority.

Let me assure you that I am a strong advocate of freedom of religion. This book attempts to graciously and accurately compare the religious beliefs of Jehovah's Witnesses with the time-honored basics of Christianity. While the reader will see that I passionately disagree with Jehovah's Witnesses central doctrines, it is not my intention to interfere with a person's right to believe as they choose. However, it is my desire that readers be aware of the danger of erroneous beliefs. Ultimately you must decide for yourself.

D.A.H.

You may contact me at:

dwighthayes3@aol.com

Contents

Dedication iii
Preface iv
Acknowledgments viii
Introduction ix
Part 1 1
   Chapter 1 Victory Over Fear 2
   Chapter 2 Father and Son 11
   Chapter 3 New Truths, New Light 20
   Chapter 4 House-to-House 33
   Chapter 5 Filled with Spirits 42
   Chapter 6 The 144,000 49
   Chapter 7 Fracturing Families 55
   Chapter 8 "Jehovah God, Please Show Me..." 62
   Chapter 9 Honey, I Just Asked Jesus..." 70
   Chapter 10 On Trial 78
   Chapter 11 I Have Decided to Follow Jesus 89
   Chapter 12 Roselie Faces the Elders 96
   Chapter 13 Farewell to Family/Family a Hundredfold
.... 103
   Chapter 14 Baptism and Discipleship 118
   Chapter 15 Reunited 127
   Chapter 16 "Dwight, Trust Me!" 132
Part 2 139
   Chapter 17 Did the Church Need Restoration? 140
   Chapter 18 Judgment and Hell 146
   Chapter 19 A Complete Savior 157
   Chapter 20 Conclusion 166

Part 3 171
   Questions and Answers 172
   Watchtower Shunning - Is it Hate-speech? 210
   What About the Pedophilia Epidemic Among Jehovah's Witnesses? 217
   Recommended Reading 220
Index 221

Acknowledgments

Roselie, my wife of forty-nine years, has loyally journeyed with me both through the tears of suffering and the unspeakable joys of victory. She is a gift from heaven. I am so appreciative for her sacrificial love. She unselfishly surrendered much of our personal time together, allowing me to work unhindered on the manuscript.

Without the assistance of Michael Abraham this book would still be in the imaginary stage. He patiently coached me, helping me put my thoughts into writing. His expertise proved both creative and practical. I will be forever grateful for his skilled services.

Long-time friend Hoyt Griffith dedicated a great many hours to studying my manuscript. He checked sources and raised pertinent questions about theological and grammatical matters. His wise counsel has been a priceless component in this project.

My son, Doug, offered suggestions on issues that needed to be especially emphasized. I am grateful for the hours he spent examining my manuscript and I appreciate his candid comments.

Above all, this book centers on the One I love most, my Lord Jesus. All praise, glory and honor be unto him.

Introduction

From ancient times, religions have punished dissident members. Some have inflicted chastisement through torture, burning and murder. Others excommunicated, shunned and disfellowshipped. Persons defecting to join a faith with contrary beliefs are the worst offenders. Sometimes these dissenters are labeled "heretics" or "apostates." Extreme measures were taken to protect faithful followers from the "corrupting" influence of these religious "turncoats." The more outspoken the defector, the more severe the consequences.

You are about to witness the story of one man's search for truth. Obedient to Jehovah's Witnesses doctrine from childhood, my earnest spiritual quest intensified as I approached my thirties. From a toddler, I had been taught that being one of Jehovah's Witnesses meant I was "in the truth."

My Witness mother instilled a deep respect in me for the Bible. I learned to accept, without question or doubt, "Bible truths" as dispensed to us by the Watchtower Society of Brooklyn, N.Y. I carried my green J.W. Bible door-to-door along with my witnessing case, packed with a variety of Watchtower publications. I read scriptures publicly before the congregation at our Kingdom Hall (Jehovah's Witnesses' meeting place) and discussed my beliefs with householders. I was certain my life was centered on the Bible's authority.

I am grateful for my strongly engrained reverence for the Bible as the Word of God. But after many years of unquestioning conformity to the Watchtower Society's teachings, I discovered within my soul a conflicted conscience. Could Mom have been wrong in her beliefs? Were we, in fact, following Bible principles as Jehovah's Witnesses claimed? Or were we unknowingly bowing to the authority of a man-made organization, espousing some ideals true to the Bible and others actually opposing the Bible. I was compelled to launch my quest for truth.

My journey took me from respected Witness leader, to conflicted questioner, and to "apostate." I was sentenced to the shame of disfellowshipping. The penalty – extreme shunning by all J.W.s which included friends and family members. As a former congregation overseer, I had also pronounced this penalty on "wayward" members of my congregation. Those who professed belief in the deity of Jesus Christ were considered particularly dangerous and worthy of our immediate judicial attention. On October 31, 1980, the penalty I had pronounced on others was decreed on me.

What had precipitated such a dramatic change in my life?

How had I discovered this truth that radically opposed my former Witness beliefs, making me too much of a corrupting influence to remain on speaking terms with lifelong friends and family? Come along with me as I share my story

Special Note: This is a revised edition of Banished. A number of important issues have surfaced since its first publication in 2011. Watchtower's Brooklyn Headquarters are being moved from Brooklyn to Warwick, NY. It may be that as many as twenty-five percent of the Bethel family (workers) have been dismissed. Watchtower and Awake! magazines are being downsized.

Also I'm familiar with a number of custody cases; JW parents are fighting non-witness parents, like never before, to control the children. In my opinion, most lawyers and judges refuse to become entangled in issues which involve religion - no matter how oppressive or dangerous a religious group can be proven to be. It appears that Watchtower expert lawyers are assisting JW parents to demonstrate parental worthiness and downplay phycological or physical damage attributed to the Jehovah's Witnesses religion, even in the face of opposing expert testimony. [As in: the JW parent refusing a life-saving blood transfusion for the child; the JW parent facing extreme shunning and eternal death by God, if he were to compromise and allow the transfusion].

More repressive measures are being implemented to insure that JW's will completely shun followers who have turned away from the Watchtower Organization. I address this issue with a new section: Watchtower Shunning – Is it Hate Speech.

Also it appears, from the media, that Jehovah's Witnesses are facing a child molestation crisis. I briefly address this topic in the section: What About the Pedophilia Epidemic Among Jehovah's Witnesses?

Modern media has uncovered Watchtower teachings that were previously hidden safely away in dusty archives. It is now possible for anyone to objectively research early Witness teachings on the great pyramid of Egypt, phrenology, and definite date-setting end time predictions. Photocopies of primary resources are no longer unattainable to the seeker.

Jehovah's Witnesses are forbidden to research or even read any religious materials other than their own literature. What is common knowledge about their religion may still be condemned by the Witnesses as "apostate lies."

Part 1

Chapter 1
Victory Over Fear

"Thou wilt keep him in perfect peace, whose mind is stayed on thee..." Isaiah 26:3 KJV

"This plane is going down!" Exclaimed Ari, the nervous passenger seated on my right.

The hulking 777 roared heavenwards, ascending noisily with Newark's Liberty Airport vanishing in our wake. I love takeoffs, thousands of horsepower propelling a massive airplane into space. "Rapture practice," I normally tell my wife Roselie, when she is seated next to me. That night, Roselie was seated two rows back.

The men to my right and left were returning home to Israel. It was May 2007, the beginning of my third Holy Land trip. In the usual tarmac chitchat, one of the men who introduced himself as Ari said he makes the trip frequently. He flies Continental, Tel Aviv to Newark. He completes his New York business, returns home to Israel's David Ben Gurion airport, travels south and homeward to Ashqelon.

"Ashqelon?" I asked, "That's getting close to those incessant rocket attacks from Gaza, isn't it?"

"Yes," he told me. His home is within range of Hamas' unguided rockets. He said the real terror is that nobody knows where the missiles are headed: perhaps a school or a market, random civilian targets.

I think about his home, his seeming insecurity, his wife's safety, and his kids' future. But now soaring hundreds of feet upward, I sensed fear in Ari's words.

Though I didn't feel any downward sensation, I wasn't the seasoned traveler, he was, he should know.

Ari moaned, "Look out the side window. See the city lights, we're headed downwards, something is wrong with this plane!"

My heart never changed pace as I prayed. I prayed in the Spirit; there was no time for speech making to God. Instantly I became enveloped with an overwhelming sense of tranquility. Sandwiched between my worried neighbors, I closed my eyes. Just bliss. Thank you, Jesus. Perfect peace.

In my first thirty-three years, death frightened me, thoughts of lying unconscious in a cold grave for a few hundred years and then maybe Jehovah God would resurrect me if he determined I had lived a good enough life.

On that evening, approaching my sixtieth birthday, bliss, not fear, overtook me. I wondered, if the plane were to spiral downward; cabin lights flickering, passengers screaming, smoke wafting everywhere, stewardesses kneeling with rosaries, would I still be overwhelmed with this otherworldly joy and peace?

I am confident God's grace is sufficient for any trial, even in the face of impending death. I was certain of entering immediately into God's holy presence, if disaster were imminent.

I had every reason to be anxious and panicky. Victory over these debilitating emotions had taken time.

From early childhood, my mother, Vera, instructed me in the beliefs of Jehovah's Witnesses. Despite my compassionate mom's best efforts, why would my early years be so heavily saturated with anxiety, joylessness, and phobias? Fear of death was at the top of my list.

Mom prepared me for kindergarten with new sneakers, rubber boots and heavy winter clothes for western New York's inevitably brutal winter. She let me choose a Hop-Along-Cassidy metal lunch box.

But for a child in a Jehovah's Witness home there was immeasurably more preparation to come. Mom spent countless hours orienting me in rules of Witness conduct. "You must never compromise," was instilled in me. It was a big word for a five-year-old and I wasn't exactly sure what it meant. I did however comprehend that it was bad, really bad. I would never compromise, because if I did, God would be angry with me. He would destroy me. I would sleep forever, others having a happy time while I slept missing blue skies and beautiful sunsets and flowers and trees. I would be rejected by God forever.

"You must never pledge allegiance to the flag," began a long list of admonitions. I didn't know anything about the flag. I only knew God didn't want me to salute it. When everyone else placed their hand over their heart and said some words, I was to stand with hands down, silent. "The Bible tells us it's wrong to worship any object. Saluting the flag is the same as worshipping it." This was a difficult concept for a five-year-old. When the teacher and the other kids would "worship" the flag, it was wrong. Even if everyone in the room did it I would not do it. God would be upset if I did it. He might destroy me forever.

I was scared but, "Okay Mom. I won't compromise. I won't salute the flag. You've told me not to, and God's organization says it is wrong. "

"And remember we don't celebrate Christmas. Nobody really knows the date Jesus was born. Besides, most Christmas songs worship Jesus. It's wrong to worship Jesus because he's not God. And don't sing Christmas carols."

It was complicated, but Mom explained over and over why Christmas was wrong. I was not allowed to draw names, exchange gifts, sing carols, say "merry Christmas," help decorate a school Christmas tree or accept holiday cookies and candy. Again, our God would be displeased if I did any of these things.

One wintry morning, when I was about six years old, Mom gathered up Christmas tree decorations, stuffed them into the wood-burning furnace, where they blazed, gone forever. Mom cleansed our home of all "pagan" Christmas objects. Just a year earlier, in 1952, she (at age 30) was baptized as a Jehovah's Witness. She had been studying with them for two years. Then she eagerly implemented Witness rules.

But Dad was not ready to give up Christmas. He grieved over the destruction of his favorite childhood holiday decorations. I recall his pained countenance that cold Saturday as black smoke curled from the chimney. To remember that scene so indelibly, I must have sensed conflict between my parents.

Mom told me her disappointing Santa Claus story. Her mother, my Grandma Allen, had always been truthful with her. But at age twelve Mom learned there was no Santa Claus. She was devastated. She was not upset that Santa was only a myth. Rather she was upset that her mother had deceived her. She told me, "I had completely trusted her, I decided then and there, to never lie to my children about Santa Claus or anything else for that matter."

When Jehovah's Witnesses first visited our house, they assured Mom that celebrating Christmas was wrong. They never lied to their kids about a Santa Claus. The Witnesses appeared to offer "the truth" about Christmas.

According to Mom they patiently answered her many questions. "Will my sons have to go to war?"

"No, true Christians don't serve in this world's armies. Jesus said his Kingdom was 'no part of this world.'"

"At church, my Universalist minister says the Bible's miracles aren't real, just illustrations, teaching a good lesson.

Do you Witnesses believe they are real?" "Yes, we believe the miracles happened."
"Do you Witnesses believe in a literal hell?"
"No. When Jesus spoke of hell, he wasn't talking about an actual fiery place, just the common grave. When people die they're sleeping, most folks will be resurrected. Really bad people, will be annihilated, that is, unconscious for all eternity. None of your relatives are in a burning hell. You have no need to worry. You'll see them again soon. They'll be resurrected, live right here on earth, helping you with your garden, enjoying life on a paradise earth, forever and ever."

Mom once told me she did not trust her minister at the Universalist Church, he, a married man, had made amorous suggestions to her, a married woman, while on a church retreat.

She felt she could trust her new friends, the Jehovah's Witnesses. Despite her trust, she was conflicted about accepting the Watchtower Society's claims of exclusivity. "I struggled with accepting the

Society as God's only spokesman between God and mankind. After two years of studying with the Witnesses, I became convinced. I was able to accept and submit to their authority."

In submitting to Watchtower authority, Mom obeyed the new rules she had learned. She cleared our home of all Christmas objects and taught her children to uncompromisingly obey our God at school. I was impressed by her convictions. Indeed, she thought she had finally found the truth. As a Jehovah's Witness, she was taught that all churches are false and an abomination to God.

I now believe Dad had bought into the ideals of 19th century religious liberalism, prevalent everywhere in the 1950's. Religion was theoretically more about feelings and emotions than doctrine. Women were supposedly more emotional, resulting in the "I-let-my-wife-tend-to-religion" mentality.

At an early age, I witnessed Dad ceding spiritual leadership responsibilities to Mom. She attended all five weekly meetings, witnessed door-to-door, instructed us kids about God, and taught us "new truths" exactly as presented in Watchtower publications. Dad was reluctant to involve himself in any Witness activities until a family tragedy swayed him towards Mom's new beliefs. Within two years, Dad would narrowly escape accidental death. But one of his sons would be lifeless.

"And Dwight, remember we don't celebrate birthdays," Mom continued her instructions for starting school. "You'll be compromising if you wish a friend 'happy birthday,' sing 'Happy Birthday,' accept a piece of birthday cake, or give or receive birthday gifts. The Bible teaches celebrating birthdays is wrong."

Within five years, Mom's parents, brother and three sisters all followed her lead, becoming baptized Jehovah's Witnesses. She had convincingly evangelized them into her new religion.

Grandma Allen always gave each grandchild a crisp one-dollar bill on their birthdays. I was delighted to get the dollar and buy ten ride tickets at the local amusement park. I once asked Mom, "Why did Grandma continue to give birthday gifts, wasn't she compromising her new Witness beliefs?"

Mom related, "It'll take a little time for Grandma to quit things she's used to doing. It'll be all right to accept the dollar a few more times."

My young mind was conflicted about this paradox. I guessed it would be okay to accept Grandma's birthday gift. Still in the back of my mind I thought I was displeasing God by compromising.

"Just as celebrating Christmas is wrong; so is celebrating any holidays wrong." Mom continued. "It's wrong to celebrate Valentine's Day. You mustn't exchange valentines or eat the cookies or candy. Likewise; Easter, Thanksgiving, New Year's Day and all patriotic holidays are wrong. Mother's Day and Father's Day are wrong because they honor people; we must honor God only."

"When the teacher leads the class in reciting the twenty-two-word State Prayer[1], just like the flag salute, you must remain silent. We pray to a different God

---

-- 1 *New York State Board of Regents prayer; discontinued in 1962* than other people. We pray to the only true God, Jehovah. Others are praying to a false god.

"Expect persecution," she predicted. "Some of the kids will hate you because you're doing what's right. Don't let that bother you. Jehovah will help you do what's right."

There was a long list of unique rules and regulations handed down to us from the Watchtower Society. We, of course, were expected to obey moral laws found in the Bible. I am grateful for my mother's insistence on obedience to moral principles.

One thing was becoming quite clear. Going to school was not going to be fun. It was going to present tough, everyday tests of obedience and stressful times for obeying our God. I nervously wondered whether I would ever compromise and make God angry.

On a chilly September morning in 1952, I heard a shout, "The bus is coming!" cried my brothers Douglas (age 11) and David (age 6). Bus #8 squealed to a halt. On this, my first day of school, they shoved me to the bus steps. Up I climbed, passing the driver, gripping the Hop-along-Cassidy lunch box tightly in my little hand. Butterflies fluttered in my stomach. I slid my five-year-old body onto a cold vinyl seat. The bus roared away, headed for a fearsome place, school. Reflected in the cloudy window, I saw the shadowy figures of Fear and Anxiety staring at me.

My reverie was interrupted by the airplane's intercom, "This is your captain. We have cleared Newark's air space. We will be landing in Tel Aviv, Israel in approximately 10 hours. You may now unfasten your seatbelts. Enjoy your flight on Continental Airlines."

Ari sheepishly glanced around the cabin, "I was wrong. The city lights had reflected in the window as the plane banked eastward, it just looked like we were going down."

I too had noticed the unsettling optical illusion. My personal reality, however, was a calmness of spirit. I had no fear or anxiety but only a sense of peace. An answered prayer and one more "rapture practice." There was a time when Ari's dire proclamation would have thrown me into a panic attack. Thankfully that had changed.

Chapter 2
Father and Son

"My son keep my words and store up my commands within you." Proverbs 7:1

"Sisu et Yerushalayim Gilu Ba," the men shouted. "Gilu Ba Kol Ohaveha," they sang joyfully, "Rejoice with Jerusalem and be glad with her, all who love her..."

Golden rays of sunlight streamed onto The Prayer Plaza. Bands of religious men skipped and danced, sang and celebrated, and carried ornate scrolls. Their blue-on-white and black-on-white striped prayer shawls swirled in the wind. Women and girls peered over the gender-separation fence, standing on white plastic chairs, and shouted congratulations and tossed candy.

It was Thursday morning. Jerusalem's Western (Wailing) Wall witnesses a twice weekly ritual of Jewish boys coming of age, turning thirteen, celebrating their entrance into manhood, the Bar Mitzvah.

Each time I have witnessed this ancient ritual, I have been deeply impressed with the strength of father-son relationships. I have wondered whether each young man will follow in his father's footsteps, take over the family business, or even pursue the same profession. And whether he will continue-on the same religious path as his father.

Fathers and sons in celebration stir memories of my relationship with my Dad. Dad and I had almost nothing in common. Dad loved farming, plowing and planting fields, harvesting dusty grain, selling wheat at the Agway mill. He liked algebra, carpentry, and basketball, but little of that rung my bell. Born June 15, 1918, my father, Verne Hayes was a middle child with an older sister and a younger brother. His father's farm bordered my mom's parents' farm, the Allen farm. Mom was born and reared next door. They married in 1940. My eldest sibling, Doug, was born in 1942. David arrived next in 1945. I was born in 1947. My sister, Vonda, in 1950.

My brother Doug shared Dad's interests; driving tractor, guarding sheep, spending nights in the field, and protecting our flock from roving dogs. Like Dad, he loved the soil. Repairing soil-tilling machinery came naturally. He amazed his shop teacher with his metal-fabricating skills. Physical strength is a must for farming. I remember seeing Doug pick Mom up and carry her around the kitchen. He was a man at age thirteen.

Doug and I sometimes hung out by a glowing campfire, watching the sheep in the moonlight. He sharpened his big Bowie knife in case a sheep-killing dog attacked. I was seven, I wanted to be like my big brother.

His interests projected far beyond his love for agriculture. Math, science, welding, converting cars into doodle bugs were just a few. By age thirteen, he had already designed and was building a manned airplane.

I sensed Dad's excitement; things were going his way. He sometimes shared his dream of farming fulltime. Soon he would leave the other jobs forever. No more would he have to make succotash and sauerkraut in the canning factory or manually shovel salt from the back of a truck during wintry nights onto icy roads for the highway department.

Mom, a frugal housewife, collected Dad's pocket change, saving twelve hundred dollars. She gave it to Dad to purchase a tractor. The slightly used, shiny green John Deere arrived on a flatbed truck and plowing had never been easier. In the spring of 1955, our fields never looked prettier. Farm life was promising.

One April evening at dusk, we were all settled in the house except for Dad and Doug who were still working with the tractor pulling big rocks out of the fields. Our serenity was suddenly interrupted by Dad's panic-stricken cries,

"Vera call the ambulance! Dougie's under the tractor!"

Somehow Mom stumbled to the wall phone, wound the crank and reached the operator. My seven-year-old heart loudly pounding, I ran after Dad one hundred yards up the hill. Behind the barn where the ground was furrowed from plowing, our new John Deere tractor laid upside-down with Doug underneath, motionless.

Darkness soon overtook dusk. Lights flashed through the windows, painting our walls red. My stomach felt sick. The night was endless. Officials came and went. Doc Howard wrote on the death certificate. "Death was instantaneous. He never suffered. Every bone in his body was crushed."

One of the last callers, a kindly uniformed man, apologized, "I'm so sorry. I know this is hard, but I need to fill out this accident report." One more time my stunned parents spelled-out Doug's full name, Douglas Malcomb Hayes, age thirteen, and our address.

Finally, in bed I laid, wide awake. Everything was quiet again except Dad, outside my window sitting in the car with the door open, sobbing. I had never heard him cry before, he sobbed loudly. Doug was gone. Dad had tried but failed to pull Doug to safety as he himself barely escaped the overturning tractor. Dad's dream was crushed.

I could not eat or sleep for days. My closest friend was dead and buried.

My surviving brother, David, also loved the soil, but his allergies were severe. He could never contribute significantly to Dad's dream. Dad later urged me towards farming. I half-heartedly tried. But the final blow was my Holstein steer, gouging me with his horns, shoving me forever away from farming. I was unsure of Doug's interest in Jehovah's Witnesses. Mom told me she had been concerned that he was not very interested in the truth. We Witnesses referred to our beliefs as "the truth." All other religions were false, we were the only true religion.

The Watchtower Society's theology promised an earthly resurrection. We expected Doug to return to us in the flesh. Likely in just months or a few years our family would reunite forever. But first the end must come. It was very close. Only Jehovah's Witnesses would survive the battle of Armageddon, the cataclysmic end of the world system. All non- Witnesses would be destroyed by God. Most of the dead, including Doug, would be resurrected to life on a restored paradise earth. All who faithfully followed Watchtower Society beliefs would be spared through the soon-coming war of Armageddon and remain on the earth. They could live forever, if they remained faithful. They would make the earth into a paradise. If at any future time, they became untrue, they would be immediately destroyed.

Dad told me that his hope of seeing Doug again moved him toward the Witnesses. He began attending some meetings, studying Watchtower literature, reading the Bible, and giving short talks at the Kingdom Hall. House-to-house witnessing, the primary task of Jehovah's Witnesses, was an insurmountable obstacle to Dad. Dad tried, but just couldn't seem to do it. We considered our house-to-house service to be a requirement in our efforts to please God, to earn his favor.

That winter (1955-1956) we spent in Florida. In southern states Jehovah's Witness maintained separate Kingdom Halls for whites and blacks. As Dad's interest in Witness beliefs grew, he often attended the "colored" congregation of Jehovah's Witnesses as it was then labeled. Dad was invited to give weekly speaking assignments. He was the only white man attending. He told me he was needed there since the group was very small. The rest of our family attended the white congregation.

Though Dad actively participated in many Witness activities, he steered clear of the most critical step, baptism. I worried he would die without being baptized. God would be displeased by Dad's disobedience and he would never be resurrected to life on earth. Dad failed to obey two of the most important steps on the path to everlasting life for Jehovah's

Witnesses, baptism and regular house-to-house witnessing.

Dad was interested in the promises of Jehovah's Witnesses, especially the resurrection. But he was reluctant to give up his interest in politics, discussing candidates, contributing to politicians, and voting, all practices forbidden by Witnesses. Witnesses argued God's people must not be involved in this world's affairs. Perhaps this is one of the reasons Dad chose to forego Witness baptism. When I later urged him toward baptism he would say, "I don't want to be a hypocrite."

As Dad had, David and I enrolled in the Theocratic Ministry School, one of five weekly meetings at the Kingdom Hall. Each Thursday night we were trained in public reading and speaking. My first assignments were reading scripture passages from The New World Translation Bible (compiled by the Watchtower Society).

From public reading, I advanced to five-minute extemporaneous talks, to later, delivering fifteen-minute talks. By age 18, I progressed to one-hour Sunday lectures.

The Ministry School was college level, equipping us to deliver an articulate and convincing message in house-to-house witnessing. As my reading and public speaking skills developed at the Kingdom Hall, I began to excel in those areas in public school. While learning the art of public speaking, the Witnesses taught me to smile as I spoke, we wanted everyone to know we were the happiest people on earth.

I learned to put a smile on my face despite a deepening gloom on the inside. As a child, I worried whether I could ever be good enough to please God. It seemed he was demanding more than I could ever give.

Would my good works be pleasing to him? Would he protect me through that awful destruction of Armageddon, the destruction that could begin at any moment? If I died before the end, would he resurrect me? Would I lie in the cold grave, unconscious for all eternity, because I had not been able to do enough to please God? I dreaded death.

Sunday talk outlines were prepared at our organization's headquarters. We were required to stick closely to the Watchtower Society's dogma, if we added personal comments on scripture we could be reprimanded. We were to avoid independent thinking. We were not "filled with spirit." Only a small group of about ten-thousand Jehovah's Witnesses were supposedly led by God's spirit.[2] We could identify these specially God-chosen persons because they alone partook of the bread and wine at our annual Memorial meeting. We were required to turn to these "spirit-anointed" ones for all scripture interpretation. Jehovah God would not want us to try to understand the Bible apart from his anointed leaders.

So, while Dad refrained from house-to-house witnessing, David and I started participating. I understood there would be no hope of everlasting life unless I obeyed God as he spoke through the organization and shared in house-to-house preaching.

When David was ten and I was eight, we began to witness house-to-house. Our first assignment was offering the Watchtower and Awake magazines for a contribution of ten cents. Most householders were

---

1 Jehovah's Witnesses do not capitalize the word "spirit" even when referring to the Holy Spirit. (see page 177) 2

kindly. Rude people emboldened us. When we faced opposition, we believed we were being persecuted for Jehovah God. We routinely spent Saturday and Sunday mornings witnessing. We spent about three hours each week in house-to-house activity. Our two-hour Sunday Kingdom Hall meeting was held on Sunday afternoon.

We turned in a weekly record of our work. "Brothers" at the Kingdom Hall made a permanent record of our field service. Based on our records we could be recommended for greater positions of congregational responsibilities.

At age eleven, I made a commitment. I remember my prayer, "Jehovah God, I dedicate my life to you.

"I sincerely wanted to please God the Father. But I doubted my ability to do so. I sensed a presence of sin in my life.

On a snowy February day in 1959 in Buffalo, New York, my brother David (age thirteen) and I were baptized by total immersion. I recall the baptizer saying, "I baptize you in the name of the Father and of the Son and of the Holy Spirit." (see Matthew 29:19,20)

As I departed the YMCA pool, I remember wondering why the baptizing brother never mentioned God's name Jehovah. This was my second baptism, the first being sprinkled as an infant in the Universalist Church in Bristol, New York. At age eleven I knew nothing of the historical Baptist struggle to win the right to refuse infant baptism in favor of believer's baptism. All I knew is that one must be old enough to comprehend the meaning of the ceremony. I did not realize Jehovah's Witnesses had adopted the practice of believer's baptism by immersion from Baptist Christians. However, unlike the Witnesses, Baptists do not teach that baptism is required for salvation. Rather a person is saved from sin by grace through faith in the name of Jesus Christ and baptism informs the world that a person has already believed and has been saved by faith. (see Ephesians 2:8,9; Acts 4:10,12).

I think Dad was pleased that David and I wanted to be religious, which would protect us from smoking, swearing, drunkenness, and other vices. Certainly, Dad tried to please Mom and he wanted to believe Doug would soon return from the grave. However, it was rumored that his dad, my grandfather, a non-Witness, was saying disapproving things in the community such as, "I can't believe my own grandsons will never salute the American flag!" I now realize Dad was a conflicted person and remained that way for most of his life.

* * * *

Returning from my moments of contemplation, I backed away from Jerusalem's old Western Wall, weaving my way through the Bar Mitzvah celebrations. Music and laughter surrounded me. Fathers and sons danced with proud grandfathers. Boys read aloud from ancient scrolls and little prayer books, preparing to accept the responsibilities of a mensch, a Jewish man.

I reflected that this kind of father-son camaraderie was absent from my past. But thanks to the Lord, I now have spiritual fellowship and blessings with my two sons, two sons-in-law, and ten grandsons, the breath of fellowship I could not have imagined as a Jehovah's Witness.

Chapter 3
New Truths, New Light

"...earnestly contend for the faith which was once delivered unto the saints. For there are certain men crept in unawares...denying the only Lord God, and our Lord Jesus Christ." Jude 3,4 KJV

On the outskirts of smog-laden Cairo, I gazed at Pharaoh Khufu's ancient funerary edifice, the Great Pyramid of Giza. All facts were impressive: archaeological, astronomical and mathematical. It is ranked as the oldest of the Seven Wonders of the World. I mentally enumerated some of the Biblical personages who undoubtedly stood on the same ground where I was standing on that November 2008 day during my fourth visit to the Holy Land.

I pictured Joseph, Jacob, Moses and the exiled Holy Family with child Jesus in Egypt, all awing at the same spectacle now looming before me.

There I reflected on Watchtower Society founder Charles Russell's interest in pyramidology (study of pyramids). He too stood in the shadow of the Great Pyramid. He inspected the Giza site in 1891 and later wrote, "The Great Pyramid of Egypt is one of God's Witnesses... whose wonderful message is a full and complete corroboration of God's plan of the ages..." (The Time is at Hand, 1907, pg. 366). Russell used measurements from within from the Great Pyramid's internal passageway. He decided that inches represent years. So many inches from the inner chamber to the pyramid's entrance, he speculated, revealed the precise year the world was to end. In particular, he predicted

1914 as the year that would commence Christ's reign over the Earth. All governmental systems were to have been destroyed before 1914, Christ's Kingdom was to be in supreme control.

Three generations after Russell, I had accepted without question every decree and end-time prediction issued from the Watchtower Society in Brooklyn, New York. The governing body of Jehovah's Witnesses called their revelations new light or new truths. New light would be revealed at our larger conventions or through the Watchtower magazine. We were taught that God continually revealed new truths to his people, Jehovah's Witnesses and those revelations would always come through his one and only earthly channel, the Watchtower organization.

In the years since 1879, the first year of the Watchtower magazine's publication, there have been a myriad of "revelations." We Jehovah's Witnesses were honored to be associated with such a progressive organization. I believed we were not stagnant in our beliefs as the churches were. Because we were in the truth, we never used the word "church." We did not want to be identified as part of Christendom. Unlike other religions, we believed God specially blessed our Watchtower leaders with superior knowledge, truths which would guide us through the trials of this doomed world.

To name a few new truths, in 1926 the witnesses celebrated Christmas for the last time. Throughout the previous 47 years they had believed they were honoring Christ by observing his birthday, just as the angels in Bethlehem had also celebrated on his birthday. But through his Watchtower channel, God instructed all Jehovah's Witnesses to abandon this practice.

Observing the Christmas holiday was then forbidden as a pagan practice.

The cross, the ubiquitous symbol of all Christianity, was imprinted on the Watchtower magazine's cover from 1891- 1931. New light after that period forbade Jehovah's Witnesses from displaying the cross symbol on Watchtower literature, wearing it on clothing or displaying it in their homes. God had "revealed" to Jehovah's Witnesses that Jesus had not died on a cross. In fact, the cross was really an ancient pagan phallic symbol, they said, and must be avoided by those in the truth. It was not merely a personal choice of conscience, but it was forbidden by Jehovah's Witnesses' leadership.

Charles Russell had a profound interest in Egyptian pyramids. They played an important role in his prophetic writings. Years after Russell's death, God supposedly revealed more new light through Russell's Watchtower successors – that an Egyptian pyramid has nothing to do with true worship. Witness leaders were attempting to distance themselves from Russell's unchristian extolment of the Great Pyramid. They rejected pyramidology, Russell's source of prophetic speculation, but continued to honor the 1914 date derived from his study of Egypt's Great Pyramid.

The Watchtower's new light had theological implications. For example, it became wrong to talk to Jesus in prayer and to worship Jesus. Gradually the title Lord prefixing Jesus' name had been almost entirely abandoned in Watchtower literature whereas early Witness books were sometimes dedicated to the Lord Jesus Christ and those early writings used the prolific Biblical words, "Lord Jesus."

Further distancing themselves from the Lordship of Jesus, Jehovah's Witnesses abandoned the traditional dating method B.C. (before Christ) and A.D. (in the year of the Lord), replacing them, in their writings, with the Christ-neutral secular B.C.E. (before common era) and C.E. (common era). One would not expect any Christian group to discard those time-honored Lord honoring dating traditions.

Our Witness friends and family would muse, "I wonder what new truths will be revealed at this summer's convention?"

We curiously looked forward to seeing what new light God would reveal to us.

In my early teens, at a Witness convention in Yankee Stadium, I recall a pleasant evening turning into a cause of apprehension when the speaker informed us that henceforth it would be wrong to stand for the singing of the national anthem. A sublime moment of being surrounded by tens of thousands of persons of like-faith turned into a panic filled night. "How will I ever survive this new light?" I wondered. Already I was faithful in refusing to salute the flag; the Watchtower Society had permitted us to stand respectfully for the pledge, silent, with hands at sides. Likewise, we had been allowed to stand silently for the singing of the national anthem. Did not Jehovah God understand how difficult it would be for me to return to an extremely patriotic school with a change in rules, making me more conspicuous than ever? This new burden, I thought nervously, would be almost too hard to bear!

The rule extended to not just the national anthem, but to all patriotic songs. Even during "God Bless America" we must remain seated. It also ruled out standing for the singing of our school's song the "Alma Mater". Additionally, we were forbidden to stand for any non-witness minister's prayer at a wedding or funeral or any other event. The explanation was simple; by standing we were showing our agreement with something which Jehovah God hated. We could still stand for the pledge because it was the additional act of placing the hand over the heart that showed agreement with the words which we thought were idolatrous.

Once as my brother and I remained seated, we were roundly and sternly scolded by our school principal. The student body scowled. Sometimes we tried to skip or arrive late at school assemblies which always began and ended with patriotic singing. On Friday, November 22, 1963 the school day was to climax with another dreaded pep-assembly. I planned to hide-out in the school's photo darkroom. It would be an agonizing experience to be caught skipping any assembly, but attending was far more painful. Suddenly outside the darkroom door I heard loud voices and weeping. The pep assembly was cancelled. Everyone was being sent home. On the bus, I was so relieved of being spared another trial that I barely contemplated the reality of the moment in history, the violent assassination of President John F. Kennedy.

New light had often filled me with anxiety and fear. Other times it had little impact on me. I recall a convention in the mid-1960's where we received new light on the resurrection. We learned that what Daniel, Jesus and Paul taught (Daniel 12:2; John 5:28,29; Acts 24:15) about the resurrection of both the righteous and the unrighteous had been previously misunderstood by our organization as well as all Bible scholars throughout the ages. Contrary to the way scripture read, there would be no resurrection of all the unrighteous. I remember discussing our new resurrection teaching with a lady about to be baptized as a Witness. She was troubled. She could not understand how we could reverse our theological view especially when it seemed to contradict scripture. I explained that our new explanation was truthful, because it came from God's anointed channel, God's sole source of truth. The prospective Witness initially objected but eventually accepted the Watchtower Society and its new light on the resurrection. She became a devout Jehovah's Witness.

Jehovah's Witnesses have long been branded as date-setters. When a Witness I was sometimes confronted by householders who rattled off a series of dates, accusing us of multiple failed prophecies. The accusation always included 1914, sometimes 1879, 1918, 1925, and 1941 were added. I dismissed accusations as being the way we used to think, our understanding had changed I argued, as God revealed new light, things were clearer now. All those dates were important, I believed, and as the Watchtower Society explained, we just did not have a clear vision of their actual meaning. Someday, we would understand the date's real significance. The year 1914 however remained a cardinal date for the Witnesses. The year Christ began his invisible rule over the earth. I would explain that even though the world's systems did not end in 1914[3] as we once had taught, some of the

---

[3] *For decades, the Watchtower Society insisted that the generation which lived in 1914 and were old enough to understand the alarming worlds events, that same generation would still be alive to witness Armageddon. Scarcely any of that 'same generation' remain; the last known WWI veteran died on February 7, 2012.*

generation living in 1914 would most certainly still be alive to witness the end, Armageddon. That explanation became more and more awkward as the 1914 generation died off.

New light came in the Society's most widely published book, The *Truth That Leads to Eternal Life*.[4] The Truth book, as we called it, discarded the same generation prophecy theory. It stated, "Although the Kingdom came into power in 1914, Jehovah did not immediately destroy those who were not serving him. How glad we can be of that! For God's long-suffering, has afforded us the opportunity to take a firm stand for his Kingdom and so escape destruction." (1981 revision, pgs. 95-96) What the Watchtower seemed to be saying was, you should be glad our earlier prophecies about 1914 failed. If they had come true we never would have been born. Now we can enjoy life and have the hope of future life on earth as explained by Jehovah's Witnesses. I overlooked those difficulties. I accepted the Watchtower Society and their explanations as my authority.

In the summer of 1967, I was asked to attend a Watchtower convention in Lewiston, Maine. I always volunteered wherever there might be a need. Once at the convention, when I had time off from my volunteer assignment, I was sitting outdoors on the grass. My thoughts on that sunny New England day were all pleasant. I thought about Roselie, the lovely pioneer

---

Florence Green was 110 years old. She was a British non-combatant service member.
[4] It was listed in the 1997 Guinness Book of Records reaching a circulation of 107,000,000 copies in 117 languages.

(full-time Witness volunteer) girl I'd met just a few weeks earlier.

Back inside the convention, disturbing words resonated from the loudspeakers. The Watchtower representative speaking was reading a manuscript talk from headquarters. The audience looked surprised by the unexpected announcement that the year 1975 would likely begin the thousand-year reign of Christ. During my twenty-year life-span, this was the first-time Jehovah's Witnesses had alluded to a new end-time date. If our leaders were prophesying correctly, the next eight years' events would include appalling trials for those of us in the truth. The world's political, commercial, and religious systems were doomed for destruction at the climactic battle of Armageddon. But despite imminent persecutions from those same systems, we Jehovah's Witnesses, if faithful in our good works, would survive the coming cataclysm and enter the thousand-year reign of Christ, on a picturesque paradise earth. Our persecutors would be exterminated by God himself.

Our studies of Watchtower Society history rarely mentioned the failed prophecies of the past. We were discouraged from an objective in-depth investigation of our religion's failures. I recollected that the Society had mistakenly thought Armageddon would occur on or before 1914. So, I was disturbed that our leaders had not learned from past mistakes, they lunged headlong into another specific year prediction for world-ending events.

Even more paradoxical, I thought, the Bible frowned on date-setting. I recalled Matthew 24:36, "No one knows about that day or hour, not even the angels in heaven, not the Son, but only the Father." Sometimes when a householder pointed out the preceding verse and questioned us as to why we had set a date for the world's end, we would rationalize, "Well the Bible says, 'No one knows the day or the hour,' but it doesn't say we couldn't know the year." (see also Acts 1:7)

In my now conflicted heart I wondered how the Society had the audacity to predict another end time date. The Bible teaches that even Jesus, the Son of God, did not know that day or hour. Did the Watchtower Society know more than Jesus and the angels?

I dared not verbalize my ambivalent thoughts, it seemed that with my head I believed the Bible to be my religious authority, but with my heart I believed the Watchtower Society to be my real authority. Until then, I accepted without question, all "new light" from Brooklyn. If I were to openly question the 1975 date or any other Watchtower teaching, I would be subjected to discipline, possibly the most dreaded punishment of all, disfellowshipping for rebellion against God and his organization. To Jehovah's Witnesses disfellowshipping is an extreme form of excommunication, it terminates all Witness relationships, both family and friends, and places one at odds with God and susceptible to destruction at Armageddon, utter annihilation, forever unconscious.

I adopted a wait-and-see attitude. In view of the Watchtower's dismal past record on date-setting and the Bible's warning against such prophecies; I was reluctant to unreservedly believe this "new truth." However, some Witnesses declined to start families because of the proximity of the end. So thoroughly convinced of the climatic 1975 date, one Witness computer programmer created job headers for all files (computer tapes) which his programs had created specifying they could expire (be written over) at the year end of 1975, his workmates caught it in time. Others sold property and entered full-time pioneer service to warn others of the nearness of Armageddon. Such full-time pioneer work might help influence God's favor and ensure survival through the end-time scenario. God would be pleased with hard-working, house-to-house preaching Witnesses. Jehovah's Witnesses experienced above average numerical growth during those "last days" preceding 1975; 1965's total of active door-to-door preaching Witnesses numbered, 1,109,806, 1975 totaled 2,179,256. Their numbers increased almost 100% during that ten-year period.

    My life seemed comparatively normal despite the impending end of the "old world." Roselie and I married in 1968. By 1975 our family had grown to four with a daughter Karrie and a son Douglas. Both Roselie and I continued to actively preach the Witness message. We did not get caught-up in end-time fervor as did some Jehovah's Witnesses.

    We were not eager for Armageddon. We felt we were not good enough to please God, thus qualifying for everlasting life on the paradise earth, nonetheless we labored along, grasping at the straws of possibility Just maybe, if there was more time left, we could improve ourselves and then with fewer imperfections, God would allow us to enter his kingdom paradise.

    The Watchtower's failed prophecies were less troubling to me than their eagerness to gloss-over mistakes. Reflecting on King David's grievous sins, he willingly humbled himself, asking for God's forgiveness. Why, I wondered, could our spirit anointed leaders not likewise admit error, saying humbly, "We were wrong." To me, the true mark of a man of God was being able to admit error and ask for forgiveness.

One more example of new light is found in the discussion of whether modern Israel's literal return to Palestine fulfills Bible prophecy.

Watchtower founder Russell was pro-Israel, believing in the promised return of Jews to Israel.[5] Russell held that a multitude of Bible prophecies regarding Israel's re-gathering were nearing fulfillment. Some of Russell's contemporaries labeled him "Zionist." Succeeding Witness leaders rejected Russell's doctrinal stance on Israel as false. The widely-circulated Watchtower publication, *Let God be True*; the same book from which my mother accepted "the truth" made these comments on Israel: "The facts and prophecies prove the natural Jews will never again be a chosen, re-gathered people." "It is a false hope that they must be re-gathered to Palestine..." These "truths" were published in the original 1946 green-cover edition, pages. 208-209. Two years after publication, on May 14, 1948, the modern state of Israel was established. Dispersed Jewish people have been and continue to be re-gathered from around the globe. How would the Watchtower Society handle their untrue prediction? Was it an admission of error? The revised *Let God be True* brown-covered edition of 1952, pg. 218, revised, "Hence the re-gathering of unbelieving natural Israelites to Palestine cannot be construed as fulfillment of prophecies." The Society is at first saying the Jews will never be a re-gathered people. Then in response to the unique return of a people scattered for two thousand years and the establishment of an Israeli state only two years after they prophesied it wouldn't happen, the

---

[5] *His view was borrowed from fundamental Christians and is a view with which I agree*

revised *Let God be True* book acknowledged the obvious return of the Jews to Palestine. But it reasoned it has nothing to do with Bible prophecy. They admitted no error.

The flow of new Watchtower revelations was a matter of fact to me, but my mistrust was building.

Returning to the present, Mona, our Egyptian guide beckoned, "Board the bus please – time to move on to the Sphinx." I wondered as I left the overwhelming presence of Egypt's Great Pyramid, did Watchtower founder Russell personally measure its interior passageway, as has been reported. Did he in fact travel here three times to see Pharaoh Khufu's tomb and why such fascination with things Egyptian? What led him to write that this monument of stone was "one of God's Witnesses?" I wondered how any religion founded on ideas bordering on occultism could ever come clean and shake off the powers of darkness.

Russell's followers honored him posthumously. They erected a 7-foot high miniature version of the Great Pyramid next to Russell's grave. I visited his grave site in 1971 while attending Witness leadership classes in Pittsburgh, PA. Our guide shared that some adherents of Russell's original teachings still visit his grave and memorial pyramid. There were numerous break-away groups that held firmly to Russell's teachings and refused to accept the new light being revealed by Jehovah's Witnesses.

New Testament writer, Jude, urged the early church to "... earnestly contend for the faith which *was once delivered unto the saints.*" (Jude 2; Italics added for emphasis) That faith was passed down by the apostles. How could the faith continue to be revealed in a succession of new light revelations by any religious group some 2000 years later?

Chapter 4
House-to-House

"Woe to you, teachers of the law and Pharisees, you hypocrites! you travel over land and sea to win a single convert, and when he becomes one, you make him twice as much a son of hell as you are." Matthew 23:15

Roselie and I arose early to wade in the Mediterranean. The rising sun silhouetted volcanic rock cliffs. On the previous evening, we had arrived in Israel's coastal Natanya. It was May 2007, the first morning of my third Holy Land tour.

Natanya lies mid-way between ancient Joppa (modern Tel Aviv) and Caesarea. As we splashed along in the morning surf, rock formations lining the shore stirred my imagination. The sea had shaped fifty-foot monolithic cliffs. I thought of Peter and his companions walking along this scenic stretch. The Bible says it took Peter two days to make the trek. According to the book of Acts, he left Joppa, embarking on a mission trip to share his faith in Christ with Gentiles in Caesarea. Peter was responding to an invitation from an Italian military man, Cornelius.

Often as a Jehovah's Witness, I felt as if I was intruding on people's lives. Unlike Peter, I was calling without invitation. Not only did we call at homes without invitation, we sometimes returned to homes where we had been asked not to come again. I recall being told many times, "Don't ever come back here again." Did we respect their request? The next time we witnessed in their community, we rationalized, let someone else go to that house. After all the householder specifically told you to stay away, so we will send someone else to their door, they did not tell that person to stay away.

Once when a teen, I told my cousin, the car captain, that I had been asked not to return to a certain house. My cousin replied, "You go ahead and go to that same house. You don't want those people's blood on your hands, do you?" In other words, If I refused another attempt to witness despite their earlier rejection, God might hold me blood-guilty, responsible for their deaths at Armageddon. I dutifully returned, and the householder again commanded me to never return. Bodily I followed the orders but in my conflicted heart I knew I had violated the Golden Rule, "Do unto others as you would have done unto you." If I had told someone to stay away from my home and they insisted on returning, I would, without doubt, be offended.

At times, I felt like I was trying to force my message on people, refusing to respect their rights to be left alone. I found it extremely difficult to witness on Christmas morning. The thought was that people were in a generous mood, likely accepting and contributing for our literature. I recall one householder's curt remarks, "Why aren't you home celebrating Christmas like us Christians?" One circuit overseer, (having oversight of 16 congregations) in defiance of the Society's instructions, told me he would not go door-to-door on Christmas morning. He did not feel right about interrupting people's intimate family time. I never witnessed in cemeteries on Memorial Day, even though it was promoted by Watchtower leaders.

Jehovah's Witnesses are best known for their house-to-house Witnessing. As far back as 1922 they were urged to preach house-to-house. Through the decades, it evolved from a voluntary activity to a moral obligation, one of several requirements to please God if one was to receive the reward of everlasting life in the "new world."

The late pop singer Michael Jackson (when still in good standing with Jehovah's Witnesses) reportedly fulfilled his witnessing obligation by disguising himself with a phony mustache and sunglasses. Rock star Prince, whom recently passed away, is likewise reported as satisfying his witnessing obligation by calling at homes with the Watchtower's message.

From age seven or eight I participated in house-to-house witnessing. Weekly meetings prepared me for this work. At meetings, we learned how to overcome or simply absorb common objections, such as "I'm too busy," or "I'm not interested," or "I have my own religion" I learned to divert the householder's train-of-thought and then get back on to my message. For example, if a person quipped, "You people have made false prophecies, how can you follow such an organization," rather than providing a thoughtful honest answer I would parrot, "That was many years ago, we are different now, lots of things have changed through the years."

I offered *The Watchtower* and *Awake*! magazines for a contribution of ten cents. At first, I was accompanied by an adult trainer. Later I went to doors alongside my brother David. In addition to house-to-house witnessing we would spend our Friday evenings doing "street witnessing," standing on busy city sidewalks, offering our magazines to passersby.

Finding hospitable people was encouraging. Folks complemented our zeal, although most disagreed with our Watchtower literature. I learned to present a short message we called a sermon. Our mantra was, "You can survive God's soon-coming destruction of this world's systems. You can live forever in a paradise right here on earth. None of your dead family members are conscious in a literal hell. You may see them again soon. In the paradise earth, God will raise them from the dead. Obey God and he may allow you to enter his everlasting kingdom."

I would attempt to read a few Bible verses to support our theology. The sermon lasted about five minutes. We concluded with a literature offer, usually a hardbound book for fifty cents. Other times we offered a subscription to our magazines or, for a dollar, our green-covered Witness Bible, the *New World Translation*.

My house-to-house experience was primarily in small towns where we witnessed along shady streets in the summer. In winter, we visited mostly rural homes; we could warm ourselves in the car as we waited our turn. Before starting out we ordinarily met for a few minutes, considered a devotional thought and prayed for God's blessing on our work. Witnesses say they are "going out in service" meaning house-to-house witnessing. They consider "field service" to be worship.

Car captains were assigned a territory. They were responsible for contacting every home on the territory map. They were expected to exhibit courageous leadership. If we pulled into a driveway with a sign reading, "BEWARE OF DOG," the captain should respond, "I'll take this house myself" rather than sending a woman or a young boy. Captains were male unless the car group was made up entirely of women, and then a woman was permitted to assume that role. On rare occasions, annoyed householders called the police complaining that we had disturbed their peace or perhaps driven on their yard. When that happened the car-captain served as group spokesman.

Car captains kept a detailed record of each householder's response. The most common objection, "I'm not interested" was recorded as "NI"; others were "B" for busy, "CA" for call again, "Bap." for Baptist, etc. The House-to-House record reminded the car captain to follow-up on any interest shown.

Our spirits were lifted by good reports. "Mr. Jones had some sincere questions about the Bible. I was able to leave the "Truth" book with him. I'm going back next week to see if I can interest him in a Bible study."

Some reports were humorous: "That lady said she has her own church. I wonder if she built it all by herself!" We all laughed. "I knew those people were hiding on me. I could see the curtains move as I approached the house. I don't look that scary, do I?" We laughed again.

Sometimes I was mistaken for long-lost relatives. "I'm so glad you came to see me again! Come in and have a seat." Once I was mistaken for their church's new pastor whom they had not met yet. "Welcome Reverend, we're so glad to meet you!" One lady cheerfully invited me in and as I got comfortable she said, "I don't mind talking with you Mormons, but those Jehovah's Witnesses annoy me like the seven-year itch."

We were somewhat to blame for the identity confusion. Rather than straightforwardly identifying ourselves as Jehovah's Witnesses, we were instructed to use pseudonyms or obfuscate to hide our true identities. "I'm a Bible student visiting homes in your neighborhood" or "I'm a missionary" or "I'm a minister."

We were taught that people would be immediately prejudiced against us if we wholly revealed our identify, but if they could just hear our wonderful message first before discovering who we were, they might be more receptive. I found this troubling because I thought God would prefer us to do his work without even the slightest deception.

The deception went further. "What are you selling?" A householder would ask. "I'm not selling anything," I would reply. "I'm offering this book for a contribution of only fifty cents." Back in the 1920's, when Jehovah's Witnesses began their door-to-door literature distribution they candidly called it "book selling." (Watchtower 1923, pp. 104, 105) In recent years Watchtower literature has, in fact, been distributed on a contribution basis. Some U.S. states demanded sales tax from the sale of literature and so the Society changed to an actual contributory system.

"You people are pacifists!" Veterans would admonish. "No, we're not pacifists," we would reply. People refusing to fight in WWII or the Korean War were not popular immediately following those terrible wars. Jehovah's Witnesses surely fit the definition of "pacifists." But we justified rejecting the then derisive title "pacifist" because we did believe in war, that is God's war, the Battle of Armageddon. By their definition, we were pacifists but by our own definition we were not.

A fellow Witness, Charles, and I once called on a young protestant clergyman. The minister said, "You are out trying to convert people!" Charles countered with our stock answer "No sir that's not our purpose. We simply bring the truth to people. They can decide for themselves whether to associate with Jehovah's Witnesses or not." The clergyman said "Now, you're really not telling the truth, are you? It is certainly your purpose to convert people." While Charles again tried to refute the gentleman, I concluded the minister was right and Charles was wrong. We were indeed trying to make converts after all Jesus instructed in scripture "Go therefore and make disciples." Charles was merely parroting the stock answer. I was repulsed by our hypocrisy.

We covered our congregation's territory frequently. The higher the ratio of Witnesses to population, the more frequently the territories got covered. Some regions populated with many Jehovah's Witnesses received visits every week. One time we covered an entire territory on a Tuesday evening. The next day we had no other territory available, so we went right back to the same houses. People complained, "You were just here last night!" None had an overnight change-of-heart. Our inflexibility was troubling to me, but my eternal future depended upon my obedience in preaching door-to-door.

I sometimes met people with serious needs; some were suffering emotional trauma, some were in failing marriages and they desired any help I could offer. We were trained to direct the conversation back to the purpose of our visit and move ahead on message. We were not trained to help people in crisis. Our advice was to start studying with Jehovah's Witnesses that would help their difficult life situations more than anything else.

Several people responded positively to my Witness preaching, accepted the Watchtower Society as God's only "channel of communication," and became baptized Jehovah's Witnesses.

House-to-house witnessing carried us into every conceivable home situation. We visited homes so filthy the car captain advised us not to go there again, bringing back to the car, in our clothes, the odor of cat feces. We witnessed to drunks, finding some amiable and others ill-tempered. Sometimes women or men displayed unusual interest in me as I spoke. They, however, had little interest in my message but likely had amorous thoughts. Our leaders wisely warned us to be cautious and not go inside suspicious places. It was always difficult approaching a homeowner surrounded by a group of his friends. He would have to humiliate me to impress his companions. Sometimes we found ourselves amid suspicious activity, such as, coming upon moonshiners on isolated dirt roads. We joked about looking like revenuers in our suits and ties.

While I was courting Roselie we spent time witnessing house-to-house. It was a good way to get to know each other. I learned the depth of her Bible knowledge, how she handled stress, and about her commitment to God and "his organization."

On a frigid day in January 1968, we were witnessing farm-to-farm in rural western New York. In other parts of the country outdoor activities would have ceased during blizzard conditions. But in that region, life went on regardless. Our driver backed into a deep snow-filled ditch near an out-of-the-way farmhouse. The farmer was not home. We were certain to suffer frostbite had we attempted to walk for help in whiteout conditions. I tried unsuccessfully placing fence posts next to the car's tires, hoping they would spin under giving us some traction. I spotted a tractor in the farmer's barn and would have "borrowed" it but for lack of keys. Finally, I convinced Roselie to enter the unlocked farm house with me and use the phone. We phoned a Witness neighbor just a few miles away. He soon pulled up on his tractor and rescued us. I was chilled-to-the-bone and caught the flu almost immediately. Roselie and her mother tenderly nursed me back to health on their living-room couch. Though I did not vocalize it, I decided then and there that I needed Roselie to take care of me, for the rest of my life.

* * * *

Six thousand miles distant and more than thirty years since our last door-to-door visit as Jehovah's Witnesses we climbed *over* the Mediterranean cliffs. A switchback led us up to the hotel. A tantalizing kosher breakfast buffet awaited us. Had Peter and his nine fellow travelers spent the night right here, I wondered? In just another day's walk he preached to a family seeking the gospel. Had that Gentile family awaiting Peter in Caesarea known that the arriving preacher had once traveled on foot with Jesus and that he and other disciples had evangelized Galilee for Christ?

Christ had instructed, "When you enter a house, first say, 'Peace to this house.' If a man of peace is there, your peace will rest upon him; if not, it will return to you... Do not move around from house-to-house." Luke 10:5-7

Chapter 5
Filled with Spirits

"Don't get your stimulus from wine (for there is always the danger of excessive drinking), but let the Spirit stimulate your souls." Ephesians 5:18 Phillips

    Midway, five miles out of Nazareth, Israel, and in route to Cana, hiking partner Jerry and I interrupted our newly begun pilgrimage to explore ancient Zippori. It was our first of four days, trekking the forty-mile Jesus Trail, twisting like an olive branch through Galilee. (October 2010) Jewish historian Josephus called the ancient capital city "the jewel of Galilee." Some scholars speculate that Joseph and boy Jesus plied their carpenter skills in Zippori.

    The sprawling archaeological site features vestiges dating before Christ, mosaics from Greek, Roman and Byzantium cultures, a classic Roman theater, and from the eleventh century a Crusader's watchtower. Amongst the dozens of mosaics, most famous is the Roman dining room floor honoring Greek wine god Dionysus. It dates to the third century. Scenes of drinking parties are surrounded by mythological bacchantes, nymphs, and satyrs. One floor scene, a masterpiece, contains more than a million tiny porcelain tiles formed in twenty-three colors. The magnum opus, a woman's portrait with a bewitching smile, head adorned with a laurel crown is touted as "the Mona Lisa of Galilee." No wonder devout rabbis were apprehensive, I thought. Zippori's Roman culture was corrupting their followers. The affluent Romans were not just having an occasional social drink – it was part of their worship. It occupied their thoughts at all times. Alcohol was one of their gods.

* * * *

As I witnessed house-to-house, sometimes folks would ask, "Are you Jehovah's Witnesses allowed to drink or smoke?" The answer: yes and no.

We were allowed to drink alcohol, in moderation. Gradually, over the years, the use of tobacco in any form was strictly forbidden. The Watchtower Society prohibited Witness farmers from growing tobacco. They were no longer permitted, even in emergencies, to assist neighboring farmers with tobacco crops.

Prior to 1973, Jehovah's Witnesses were permitted to smoke or cultivate tobacco, but new light from the Society revealed this to be an offense punishable by disfellowshipping. It was explained that tobacco was used during worship of false gods – like the Indian peace-pipe ceremony. Smokers, we were told, were opening themselves up to demonic influence, literally sorcery.

Even before associating with Jehovah's Witnesses my family was teetotaling and tobacco-free. The conviction was not religious but traditional. There was no alcohol in our house that I knew about. Our closest Witness friends however were cordial grape growing Italians. So, my first memory of being around alcohol was at congregation picnics where our Italian acquaintances shared their homemade grape wine. Mom and Dad softened their abstinence stance a little. The Watchtower Society allowed drinking in moderation, therefore it must not be as evil as they had previously thought. They became less judgmental toward imbibers. Nevertheless, our parents remained abstainers and I was reared in a dry environment. Mom continually warned me of inevitable disaster if I ever were to start drinking.

Great Grandma Tilley stayed with our family in her last years. She was preternaturally grouchy. Her disposition greatly improved when she accompanied us to wine-flowing congregation picnics. Mom was unexpectedly pleased to see Grandma Tilley in a cheerful state of mind even if only at those wine-imbibing congregational events. Nonetheless Mom sometimes complained about new Witnesses being "initiated" into an alcohol drinking culture as soon as they became associated with our congregation. It seemed to trouble her that becoming a Jehovah's Witness was nearly synonymous with alcohol use.

Watchtower founder Pastor Charles Russell was an opponent of alcohol. He believed prohibition was best for our country. The second Watchtower president, "Judge" Rutherford (died 1942) had no such scruples against liquor. There were few restrictions on moderate alcohol consumption at the Brooklyn, world headquarters, Bethel (meaning "House of God") during the leadership of Rutherford and succeeding presidents.

At age sixteen I visited a friend serving at the Brooklyn Bethel home. Though weary from travel, I joined him and several hundred Bethelites already in a meeting. I was hot in my big winter coat, famished after traveling seven hours from western New York, and frazzled by Big Apple traffic. I felt lightheaded. I rose from my chair, heading towards the auditorium exit-door, searching for a lungful of cool air. I recall grasping a metal door handle. Everything went black. I must have smacked my head on the corner of a wooden planter as my body yielded to gravity. As I woke several kindly brothers were tending to my battered forehead.

Still feeling woozy, one of the men said, "You need to raise your blood pressure, I have just what you need, here's a shot of whiskey." I felt better immediately. I was grateful for their assistance. Bethel was the last place I expected to get my first taste of liquor.

My Bethelite friend had been there only a few weeks, he enjoyed his work assignment and he was honored to be in close proximity of the governing body. With a Band-Aid on my head, I received an insider's tour of the Bethel home. It housed staff and workers who at the nearby Watchtower factory manufactured millions of hardbound books and magazines each month. Back in his dorm room, with a sparkle in his eye, he showed me his liquor stash. I was taken aback. I had no clue that he had such a keen interest in alcohol. It was what I would have expected of a "worldly" student entering a secular college, not of a "dedicated brother" accepted into Jehovah God's service in such a sacrosanct place.

Because I came from a tee-totaling family, I grew up with a more negative view towards alcohol than many other Jehovah's Witnesses. My friend went on to explain that while he was permitted reasonable use of alcohol, Bethelites had been recently warned to be more discreet in disposing of their empty containers. The leaders conjectured that a mountain of empty booze bottles would be a poor testimony to the garbage collectors. It would be best if my friend and the hundreds of his Bethelite comrades would find alternative ways to dispose of their empties.

One evening in the early 1960's, the new Congregation Overseer (pastor) visited our home. He had been assigned to us from Watchtower Farms, an agricultural complex near Ithaca, New York. The food grown at the farm fed the Bethelites in Brooklyn. Mom said she could tell he'd had a few drinks, perhaps at his previous home visit. "He had a 'glow' from drinking wine," she said. I wasn't sure what that meant. He was jovial and personable, qualities I liked in a leader. I did see him mistake a window for a door when he was ready to depart. Mom had to show him the proper way out. Having never consumed alcohol I could not comprehend Mom's negative reaction. My opinion of our new Overseer remained positive.

For our fifth anniversary, Roselie and I traveled to Watchtower conventions in England and Belgium. Witness conventions are family-oriented with children attending. At the Brussels convention, our Witness-operated refreshment stands were selling sandwiches and cold beer to conventioneers. There appeared to be no age limit for alcohol consumption. By this time (1973) I had accepted the Witnesses' use of alcohol as normal and socially acceptable.

Gradually, despite my teetotaling upbringing, I became an imbiber. A few drinks made an otherwise boring evening endurable. I began to fellowship with Witness friends who enjoyed social drinking. Alcohol seemed to ease my anxieties; it inflated my courage. A fellow elder and I became drinking buddies. We could share our deepest thoughts with no fear of breaking confidence. Committed to moderation, we would first decide on some distinguishing point on the Jack Daniel's label. When the whiskey level got down to that point we abstained from further imbibing. We usually chased down our whiskey with beer.

After an elder's meeting, if we met in a home, sometimes our host would provide snacks and alcoholic beverages. We would stay an extra hour or so for fellowship. Some elders were abstainers, one told me beer made him mean so he stayed away from it. I thought the abstainers were a little stressed out and that it might be good for them to loosen up a bit, they reminded me of petulant Great Grandma Tilley. A little wine had made her heart glad.

As presiding congregation overseer, I attended a rigorous two-week training seminar in Pittsburgh called Kingdom Ministry School. I recall an interesting comment made by our esteemed instructor. He was teaching on the divine inspiration of the Bible. He also listed other sources of inspiration. He said music, beautiful scenery, a lovely woman, and alcohol had all provided inspiration for secular literature. I thought of Edgar Allen Poe, his reported use of drugs and alcohol and his macabre writings. Through the years, I honestly wondered if some of the Watchtower's unsettling notions came through the inspiration of alcohol rather than by divine inspiration.

My use of alcohol increased to a point where my wife said, "I don't think you can live without it." I replied, "Of course I can live without it!" while knowing in my heart she was right. Later I will present my feelings of being overwhelmed with anxiety and fear. The most courageous act in my life will be without the aid of alcohol. Thankfully, my alcohol dependency would subsequently come to an end in the twinkling of an eye.

* * * *

With ancient Zippori miles behind, Jerry and I, thirsty and hot, finally plodded into Cana village. A small boy greeted us, "Are you looking for the Cana Wedding Guesthouse?" We followed the lad up the street, through a villa gate and finally up stone steps. The boy's mother welcomed us with ice cold lemonade.

In anticipation of our arrival, she had prepared the refreshing beverage from lemons grown in her yard.

Our room lay across the street from the chapel marking the site where Jesus turned water into wine. Unlike Zippori's idolatrous obsession with wine, here in Cana, Jesus turned water into wine to celebrate a festive wedding, the first of his many miracles

Chapter 6
The 144,000

"Do not be afraid, little flock, for your Father has been pleased to give you the kingdom." Luke 12:32 "I have other sheep that are not of this sheep pen. I must bring them also. They too will listen to my voice, and there shall be one flock, and one shepherd." John 10:16

One of my favorite Holy Land sites is Nazareth Village. I am generally not interested in recreated settlements, but Nazareth Village is an exception. The site lies in a district of Nazareth thought to be similar to where Jesus grew up. By providence it could be the exact site, but of course no one knows.

The village features a synagogue, first-century style houses, grain field, vineyard, winepress, olive press and a watchtower. Re-enactors perform live demonstrations of vocations and crafts from two thousand years ago. On my last visit, I spent a few moments greeting the shepherd tending his little flock. I wanted to get to know him. How long has he worked there? Does he have a family? Did he actually grow-up caring for sheep?

From childhood, I was taught at the Kingdom Hall that Jesus had a "little flock," but I could never be one of that flock. That privilege was reserved exclusively for 144,000 special persons. They alone would get to know Jesus the Good Shepherd. They would someday know him personally. They must remain faithful to Jehovah God and his earthly organization until death and then they would proceed to life in heaven with Jesus.

I, and the vast majority of Jehovah's Witnesses, were "sheep" of a secondary flock. We were called the "other sheep class."[6]

I was repeatedly asked this question as I witnessed house-to-house, "You Jehovah's Witnesses say only 144,000 go to heaven. Your members number in the millions. What about the rest of you? Don't you feel sad you're not going to heaven too?" It's a logical question for Christians to ask, after all, Christians talk about heaven and sing a multitude of songs about knowing and seeing Jesus.

My programmed answer was, "Jehovah's Witnesses, as a majority, have an earthly hope. We desire to live forever, not in heaven, but on a paradise earth." I was always taking in knowledge about Jesus, I thought I knew a lot about him. I was taught that he was "a god." (John 1:1 *New World Translation*) While living on earth he set a fine example for us and in the future, he would reign invisibly over the earth with the 144,000. But I had no desire to be with him because I didn't personally know him. Why would I want to spend eternity with someone I did not really know? Someone I was forbidden to talk to in prayer. I was certain that those of the 144,000-class had somehow been called to heavenly life and that they "knew" Jesus in some special way. Supposedly God's spirit would bear witness with their spirits, letting them positively know they were of the special heavenly class. I viewed "the calling" of the 144,000 as a special privilege, they would know Christ personally. I did not. Again, I had no

---

[6] *Many Bible scholars interpret the Biblical passages in Luke 12:32 and John 10:16 as meaning that the "little flock" represents Jewish followers of Christ and "other sheep" represent Gentile believers.*

desire to be with someone I did not know, but I assumed that these favored ones eagerly awaited seeing Christ and heaven.

While I was serving as presiding overseer (pastor) in the Franklinville, New York Congregation of Jehovah's Witnesses, I invited a family friend to deliver the Sunday lecture. I knew that Homer Wright claimed to be "of the heavenly class." His future hope was to go to heaven. I specifically asked him to speak on the subject of how he and others of the little flock knew they were going to heaven.

Before retiring to Florida, Homer had been a long time presiding overseer in that same Franklinville Congregation, my wife's home congregation. I first met him in my preteen years. It was through the Wrights that I later met Roselie. Brother Wright performed our marriage ceremony in 1968. It was a special honor to know him and others of the "heavenly class." Of the nearly 2-1/2 million Jehovah's Witnesses in 1970, they were only 10,526 [7] self-identified Witnesses remaining with the "heavenly hope." They are not nominated or appointed but they believe they are called by God. The vast majority of the little flock (the 144,000), spanning the preceding 2000 years, had already died and risen to heaven, so we thought.

Mr. Wright titled his Sunday lecture, "Those Called to God's Heavenly Kingdom," which he delivered on July 25, 1971. In anticipation of the extraordinary opportunity to hear one of God's anointed speak on the

---

[7] *Surprisingly the number of those remaining has not been decreasing. In 1970 there were 10,526 claiming to be of the 144,000. Forty-one years later in 2011, there were 11,824. Seventy-six years have passed since the 1935 cutoff date.*

how and whys of his heavenly hope, I recorded his lecture on my cassette tape recorder.

Homer preached the official Watchtower teaching. "Starting with the apostles until now there have been only 144,000 Christians chosen to enter heaven," he said.[8] "The Bible was written primarily for these. Those, of this class, are the only ones Jesus refers to as being "born again" [John 3:3]. All those called by God [belonging to the 144,0000] were called by 1935." Homer had developed an interest in the Watchtower's doctrines back in 1918 and associated himself with Jehovah's Witnesses before 1935.

Homer explained that anyone in recent years claiming to be of the "heavenly class" is either mistaken or they are in fact replacing unfaithful "remnant members" (yet another name for those remaining) who lost out because of being unfaithful to God and his organization. Those of "the heavenly class," also called "the anointed," know there're going to heaven because they were "in the truth" (associated with Jehovah's Witnesses) before 1935. When reading the Bible, "the anointed" believe it speaks directly to them because it was written especially for them.[9]

---

[8] The Watchtower Society interpreted the number 144,000, found twice in the Bible's concluding book, "The Revelation", to be the number of those resurrected to dwell with Christ in Heaven. The resurrected of this group happened in 1918 they said. Those of this group dying between A.D. 33 and 1917 unconsciously awaited the 1918 resurrection. Contrariwise many Bible scholars view that number in Revelation as the literal number of future Christianized Jews called to preach the Gospel worldwide just before Christ's return (see Revelation 7:4 and 14:1)

[9] "New Light" presented at the 1935 Watchtower convention in Washington D.C. revealed that Jehovah's Witnesses would no

As Homer spoke, I was particularly perplexed by one comment. "It transcends all human ties, they know they're prepared to die and the ones left behind are conscious that they're never going to see these [of the 144,000] anymore...husband, wife, children, grandchildren; he knows he's going to give up all those earthly natural ties forever. So, since it's a natural hope to live on earth, that's the way God made us, those who are called to the heavenly kingdom are really making a sacrifice."

While I had no desire to go to heaven, how, I wondered could anyone think going to heaven was a sacrifice? I had also heard other anointed Witnesses speak of their sacrificially giving up earthly life to go rule over the earth with Jesus in heaven forever separated from family. How could anyone think that being part of this special little flock of only 144,000, who would enter into the awesome presence of Holy God and reign with Christ to be a sacrifice? How could such a great honor be called a sacrifice?

Almost exactly nine years later, I would know for certain whether my destiny was to be life on earth or eternal bliss in heaven with the Good Shepherd, Jesus.

* * * *

---

longer be searching for those of the "little flock", their number being complete. From 1935 on they would be seeking "other sheep" whose hope would be ever-lasting life on earth. Conversely many Bible scholars teach that a restored paradise earth awaits following the return of Christ. Those populating the earth will be survivors from a time of great tribulation. Christian scholars believe that all persons now believing in the name of Jesus Christ know Him and will join Him in heaven and rule upon the earth. (Revelation:)

Back to 2010, my conversation with the shepherd in Nazareth Village was very brief. I want to get more acquainted with him, learning more about him as he tends his little flock, perhaps communicating with him by email. I would like to know him personally. Next trip, I want to ask him what he thinks of the Good Shepherd from his same town, Nazareth

Chapter 7
Fracturing Families

"I [Saul] persecuted the followers of this Way [Christians] to their death, arresting both men and women and throwing them into prison... and went there [Damascus] to bring these people as prisoners to Jerusalem to be punished." Acts 22:4,5

"Hey, here's the Roman Road!" Fellow hiker Jerry pointed ahead. It was the second day of our forty-mile, four-day trek on Galilee's Jesus Trail. (see Chapter 5) Early that morning we had ascended out of Cana, walked a balmy eucalyptus-lined ridge, and descended to the Golani Junction, where two major Israeli highways intersect. But the Israelis were not the first to construct a highway there; just a few hundred yards ahead lie the remnants of an ancient Roman road.

Our Jesus Trail guide book suggested, "... it is difficult to know the exact location of ancient routes, Paul [Saul] may have been walking this road when he experienced his life-changing encounter with Jesus." (*Hiking the Jesus Trail*, pg.86)

Paul was ruthless. He arrested, bound with chains, and participated in the killing of Jews who claimed to follow the crucified rabbi, Jesus of Nazareth. Their crime? Apostasy. They had professed faith in Jesus Christ, the man from Galilee who had claimed to be Messiah, never denying that he was Divine. Perhaps it was on this very Roman road that Paul intended to drag his bound victims to Jerusalem to stand trial.

* * * *

Back in March 1976, I got word that a Jehovah's Witness couple was professing faith in Jesus Christ. I immediately determined to find out their thoughts about Jesus. I needed to know what they were publicly saying about Jesus. I summoned them to a "judicial hearing" before a committee of three Witness elders.

"Does this mean you now believe in the Trinity?" I wryly asked the couple on trial in front of me. Judy and Gary had been devout Jehovah's Witnesses. Judy was a fulltime pioneer worker, as her parents had faithfully raised her in the truth. Her husband was a Witness elder. The handsome mid-thirties couple had answered our request to appear before the Canandaigua, New York Congregation's Judicial Committee. As presiding overseer of that congregation, I chaired the committee.

I looked into Judy's sparkling brown eyes awaiting her reply. "I don't know how to answer that question; all I know," she unpretentiously replied, "I asked Jesus to come into my heart... now I have this peace I've never had before."

Somewhere deep in my soul I was struck with envy, telling myself that I did not have the same peace I saw in Judy. Stymieing that notion, I tersely continued, "If you believe in the Trinity and claim to be born again, you know what we'll have to do, don't you?"

She replied soberly but confidently. "Yes. We expect to be disfellowshipped." Both Gary and Judy seemed equally committed to their new beliefs.

I sometimes wondered why people like Judy and Gary would even respond to the elders' demand and show up for trial. Not all did. A few years later I would come to appreciate their motive.

To Judy's Witness parents, disfellowshipping would signal forced disassociation with their daughter and son-in-law. Our Watchtower leaders warned that if any turned away from the truth to follow another religion he or she must be considered apostate. Judy's parents would no longer be allowed to speak with their only child and her husband. They would however be allowed to communicate with their grandson and granddaughter, surely an awkward relationship. The grandchildren had not been baptized as Jehovah's Witnesses, they were not guilty of turning away from the truth. They were not apostates.

Witnesses found guilty of egregious behavior such as apostasy were expelled to keep the congregation pure. "One rotten apple ferments the whole barrel."

Furthermore, disfellowshipping would spell spiritual death for the offender. God would destroy unrepentant persons at Armageddon. If the evildoer were to die before "the end," he would never be resurrected but remain unconscious for all eternity. The Judicial Committee and I believed we had the serious responsibility of determining whether-or-not errant Jehovah's Witnesses were placing themselves in defiance of God and his earthly organization. We sought their humble repentance. But all too often the severest form of discipline had to be administered: disfellowshipping. Every Witness shuttered at the very mention of that word.

Of all infractions, apostasy was the most reprehensible. We did disfellowship for ungodly practices such as fornication, adultery, drunkenness, thievery and other infractions which the Watchtower Society deemed "unbecoming conduct." Those Witnesses accused of misconduct were given opportunity to repent. Unrepentant Witnesses could not simply withdraw from association but would necessarily be disfellowshipped. For less serious wrongdoings there were lesser forms of discipline like "private rebuke" or "public rebuke." Gossiping for example would not be considered a disfellowshipping offense. It would likely require some form of rebuke.

From time-to-time the Society issued new light on sexual conduct between husbands and wives. When oral sex was condemned, one couple chose to voluntarily confess to the committee their difficulty in giving up the practice. As a committee member, I felt embarrassed as I sat in on the conversation, however I was loyal to God's organization. I followed Watchtower instructions on how to deal with such situations.

Our list of infractions extended into other areas too. Observing holidays, celebrating birthdays, willingly permitting a blood transfusion, or being party to an organ transplant between the years 1967-1980; all were punishable offenses. Sometimes the Society would reverse an earlier ruling. After a twelve-year prohibition, organ transplants were again allowed, a reversal that dramatically impacted my family as I shall illustrate later.

Mom's sister, my Aunt Jean, was disfellowshipped for participating with her non-Witness husband in Christmas activities in their home. Sadly, it splintered our extended family, composed almost entirely of Jehovah's Witnesses. My grandmother seemed to never recover from the agony of separation between herself and Jean.

One time I led the committee in disfellowshipping a long-time Jehovah's Witness. His wife had died of cancer and he then married a Baptist woman. He compromisingly allowed his new wife to hang Christmas decorations in their home. He, being the "head of the house" bore responsibility for permitting this "evil activity." He refused to repent. Our only alternative was disfellowshipping.

We disfellowshipped another man for a theological variance. He insisted, according to Revelation 5:10, the 144,000 "heavenly class" of Jehovah's witnesses would rule literally on the earth for a thousand years. He argued that most all Bible translations used the phrase "on the earth" unlike the Jehovah's Witnesses Bible which rendered the phrase "over the earth." The difference between the two words "over: and "on" is dramatic. Christ, ruling over the earth allows for an invisible reign from heaven as taught by Witnesses. Ruling on the earth allows for mankind to visibly see Jesus, a thought not compatible with Watchtower doctrine. The Bible appeared to back the man's argument. Clinging to the Bible verse, he refused to recant, we disfellowshipped him, not for being unbiblical but for refusal to accept the Society's interpretation of scripture. We were "in step" with the Watchtower organization, even though Witness doctrine at times seemed to contradict the Bible.

Generally, Jehovah's Witnesses would not allow anyone to withdraw voluntarily from the congregation. Some Witnesses moved far away and failed to transfer their "service records" to a new congregation. If we thought there was any possibility of wrongdoing, we would investigate and try to deal with the departing Witness. Sometimes cold cases were reopened because we believed unresolved wrongdoing could limit Jehovah's spirit and blessing upon his congregation.

Our Judicial Committee "mercifully" allowed Gary and Judy a few days to reconsider the grave consequences of their apostasy. When they refused to repent, we disfellowshipped them.

We composed and read a short letter to the Canandaigua Congregation. "We the Judicial Committee disfellowship Gary and Judy A. for conduct unbecoming a Christian." We notified other local congregations, so they could likewise inform their people. Gary and Judy must be avoided. It would be wrong to pray for their restoration. Witnesses always heeded the shunning warnings. If any Jehovah's Witness were to disobey the disfellowshipping order, he or she too would first be cautioned and then if unrepentant, disfellowshipped for fraternizing with ex-Witness "evildoers".

All disfellowshipping actions were subject to the approval of the Society. Details of each case were kept on file at the Brooklyn headquarters. The disfellowshipping actions I implemented were never appealed by the offender nor were they ever challenged by the Society. Those disfellowshipped could apply for reinstatement after they had repented and were willing to attend all Kingdom Hall meetings for a year. This was exceedingly difficult since they were ignored while at those meetings for even a simple greeting was forbidden. Finally, we would consider their request to return. The path to reinstatement proved insurmountable for most disfellowshipped Witnesses. I recall people applying for reinstatement, but lacking the courage and fortitude to "make it back" into fellowship. On very rare occasions some succeeded.

Shunning through disfellowshipping created a personal crisis of conscience. A family friend, a Jehovah's Witness, used to drive my brother David and me to Rochester's new car shows. The Watchtower Society warned that all churches were false and controlled by the devil. We were not allowed to enter a church for any religious program. I think our kindly friend may have missed gospel music, music not allowed at the Kingdom Hall. He was caught exiting a church; he was disfellowshipped. Once I saw him walking toward me on my side of the street, I quickly crossed to the opposite side to avoid him. If we had come face-to-face, I would not be allowed to utter even a simple greeting. I felt as though I was obeying God and his organization, but my conscience felt pained.

The next time I saw Judy and Gary was five years later and a thousand miles away under balmy Georgia skies. How would they greet the man who fractured their family and bound them with the chains of disfellowshipping?

* * * *

Back in Israel hiking the Jesus Trail I meandered among large boulders which had once paved the Roman road's top layer. A cloud providentially moved in place over us, shading through Galilee's hottest hours.

Had Paul headed towards Damascus on this ancient highway? Was it on this same Roman road where his life was forever changed? Where when blinded by a brilliant light he cried out to the Lord Jesus, becoming a disciple of Jesus of Nazareth? Arriving in Damascus, as a new believer, Paul was greeted by those he had persecuted, at first with suspicion and then with love and acceptance.

Chapter 8
"Jehovah God, Please Show Me..."

"Ask and it will be given to you; seek and you will find; knock and the door will be opened to you." Matthew 7:7

"Watch your step!" "Please watch your step as you board!" cried the crew in yellow rain slickers. My wife and I huddled in a squally rain, clinging to our flimsy ponchos. I wondered if nature would spoil our first Sea of Galilee voyage (November 2005). The old wooden boat listed side-to-side. Waiting our turn, we at last cautiously climbed into its shifting hull; we joined thirty-one fellow pilgrims.

Thinking of Jesus commanding storms to cease, right here on these same waters. I declared to Roselie, "Just imagine! Sailing on the Sea of Galilee in a storm."

I later learned that because of its juxtaposition with the Dead Sea (hot air) and Mount Hermon (cold air) the Sea of Galilee experienced sudden and sometimes violent storms. The opposing air masses battled high in the atmosphere, creating below, white-capped waves and howling winds. That day, our Israeli crew was navigating through a small wet gale. But with near zero visibility; the blowing rain soaked everyone, even under the boat's canopy.

Galilee's storm reminded me of my own life's storms. Now looking back to the spring of 1977, I recall the dark clouds of fear and doubt rising, a foreboding voyage seemed to lie ahead.

Sitting at my friend's kitchen table, I listened as he spoke. "It's one thing to drift away and quit being one of Jehovah's Witnesses. But this thing about leaving the "truth" and becoming a "born againer" ... I just can't go along with that at all!" My fellow elder and drinking buddy murmured as he chased his Jack Daniels whiskey with a swallow of Schlitz beer. "It's just too hard on your mother, when you turn away and become a damned apostate!" He was angry at Gary and Judy's decision to leave the truth for the worst of all reasons, joining up with those despised born-again Christians.

My friend's remarks startled me. I wondered if he had been considering leaving the truth, something I was confident I would never do. And never would I turn apostate like Gary and Judy, dishonoring and breaking the heart of my faithful Jehovah's Witness mom by being dis-fellowshipped. Even more significantly how could I disobey God by joining another religion? After all, I thought, all other religions are false and demon-inspired.

While I expected to be forever loyal to the Watchtower organization, my conscience swirled like a storm over the Sea of Galilee. The Society sometimes illustrated loyalty to the organization metaphorically. They spoke of Noah being protected, safe and secure in the ark during the watery destruction of an ancient world. It was like staying within the Watchtower organization they taught, if I remained in God's modern-day "ark" or organization, I too could remain safe and secure through all this world's storms.

But my barbed conscience stirred waves of doubt. Were all other religions really of the devil?

Jehovah's Witnesses were not allowed to enter churches to attend services. I was exempted since my profession of a wedding photographer required that I go into churches to take photos. I would go inside the church building as a service to the bridal couple, not to participate in "false worship." But I found myself eavesdropping on the service as the soloist stood up and sang "The Lord's Prayer." The words were straight out of the King James Bible.

We would not sing "The Lord's Prayer" at the Kingdom Hall, it would be too ritualistic, too churchlike. Nor would we use the word "church." We had to remain separate from Satan's false religions which included Christendom's churches.

Starting in the late 1960's I photographed weddings. As "The Lord's Prayer" was beautifully sung, always something deep inside me stirred. I felt faint but wonderful chills. The singer's voice rose in crescendo into the last but most sublime stanza, "For Thine is the Kingdom and the power and the glory, forever. Amen." Why did I sense a feeling as if something holy was surrounding me? Could there be something worthwhile in the churches after all?

In house-to-house service people sometimes offered me their church literature, I was not allowed to accept it. I would perhaps say a polite "No thank you." I was too embarrassed to honestly say "We're not allowed to accept your church magazine." I did not want the householder to think we were narrow-minded. Reading any religious literature not produced by the Watchtower Society was strictly forbidden. It could delude and pull Witnesses away from the organization, God's only ark of safety.

Our organization's censorship was reminiscent of the Roman Catholic "Index," the infamous list of books forbidden to Catholic readers. But the Vatican II Council annulled the "Index" in 1966, allowing Catholics to freely choose their reading. Meanwhile the Watchtower Society tightened its censoring grip. Catholics were given more freedom while Jehovah's Witnesses were losing theirs due to increasingly authoritarian leaders. It just didn't make sense. Jesus said the truth will set you free. How could reading anything cause one to break loyalty with his firmly held convictions?

Adding to the perfect storm of my conflicted conscience was the 1975 prophecy failure. 1975 had come and gone. I was both relieved and disturbed that the Watchtower Society's 1975 prediction had failed (see Chapter 3). I was relieved because I'd lived 28 healthy years, had a beautiful wife and thus far two children and loved my work as a photographer. We were surrounded by family and loyal friends. I held responsible leadership positions within our local congregation. I prayed and hoped that my "works of righteousness" were pleasing to God. I didn't yearn for a cataclysmic change. On the other hand, I was disturbed that the Society had misguided us in a litany of failed predictions. I could only think of one prophecy that had, indeed, come to pass. Back in the 1920's the Society had not predicted the date of its demise, but successfully predicted the eventual failure of the League of Nations. Surely many secular prognosticators also foresaw the League's downfall.

Worse yet, after raising the expectations of many Jehovah's Witnesses, the Society was unwilling to humble themselves and admit failure. I began to question whether they were divinely or humanly directed. If I expressed my skepticism openly, my conflicted conscience might lead to disfellowshipping.

As my spiritual struggles continued, a move offered a new beginning.

Western New York's winter of 1976-1977 was brutal. Roselie and I had always found cold weather painful. My brother enjoyed snowmobiling and my sister skied cross-country. Unlike me they faced winter with a measure of delight. February blizzards piled a seven-foot hard-packed snowdrift in our driveway, the kind movable only by backhoe. "Honey, there must be a warmer place to live," I shivered from the bitter wind as I dug away with a pointed shovel, "Why don't we visit your sister in Virginia? The winters there must be milder."

By October 1977 we were living in the foothills of Virginia's Blue Ridge Mountains where winters are 15 degrees warmer and are blessed with far less snow.

The Rocky Mount, Virginia, Congregation of Jehovah's Witnesses warmly welcomed us. The majority of their leadership had also moved in from northern climates. They saw in me another elder, public speaker and perhaps committee member. But I saw the opportunity to step back and think about where my life was headed.

A rarity in the Rocky Mount, Congregation was the presence of three Witnesses who professed to be of the chosen 144,000. Most congregations had no members of that special group. My fellowship with one of these fine people led me to question my faith even further. He explained his calling at a book study group. Like my friend, Homer Wright (see Chapter 6) his calling as one of the 144,000 was dependent upon the timing of his affiliation with Jehovah's Witnesses. He did not explain it as does the Bible. Paul writes, "The Spirit himself testifies with our spirit that we are God's children" (Romans 8:16). While my hope was to live on the earth forever, I sensed that anyone providentially chosen for heavenly life must have more than a date when they became a Jehovah's Witness to present as evidence. There must be some evidence within their heart and soul.

I had never searched for truth, I had been confident I was already "in the truth." No further exploration was needed. But now my attitude was changing. With diminished confidence in the Society my earnest search began.

I recall the last time I went house-to-house as a Jehovah's Witness. It was in Glade Hill, Virginia. The housewife said, "My husband would really like to talk to you." I sensed from her tone, her husband probably wanted to witness to me about his faith. She invited me to return that Sunday afternoon.

Ordinarily I would have prepared myself to debate the Trinity with a born-again Christian. But this time I wasn't thinking about debating anyone. I was honestly ready to listen to another religious viewpoint. "Perhaps they have what I need," I thought. When Sunday came, I alone drove to the house, nervously anticipating what might happen. I knocked hesitatingly. No one answered. I was relieved but disappointed at the same time; I had mustered the courage to search, but my first attempt proved fruitless. I was aware of a spiritual need in my life, it was no longer being satisfied by Jehovah's Witnesses. I had even lost faith in the highly respected anointed remnant of the 144,000. I was not sure, but I had hoped that the man at the Glade Hill house could share something to satisfy my spiritual hunger, something so real and powerful that if necessary I would give up all to attain. That hope was fading in my rearview mirror. I returned home empty.

The thunderous storm of guilt would not blow away. How could I have split up families in the name of God and truth? Jehovah's Witness friends detecting my "drifting," sincerely tried to encourage me, urging me to get closer to Jehovah God by drawing closer to his organization, an organization I now reasoned was hurting more than helping people. Others warned me not to doubt God's organization, after all, continued questioning might lead to a fearful consequence, dreaded disfellowshipping. Then where would I go to?

Where would my doubts take me? Could it be that my primary mentor, Mom, had been deceived all along? Alcohol provided temporary relief from my despair, but I needed something more soothing than Southern Comfort, a friend closer than Jack Daniels.

Often at night I would kneel by our bed to pray. Usually my prayers had been quite general, like "God please protect all your Witnesses throughout the earth, spare them from persecution and please watch over your organization..." That night in the spring of 1980, I remember praying specifically "Jehovah God, you say in your Bible if I keep on asking, I will receive and if I keep on knocking, the door will be opened. Jehovah God, please show me the real Truth, if it's Jehovah's Witnesses I will try to be the best Witness for you, but if it's something else please show me." With all my heart, I expected an answer from heaven.

* * * *

Now twenty-five years later, I was in a significant rain storm, Israel's rainy season had begun early. As we rocked on the stormy sea our host, Micah, conducted a wedding ceremony, a couple married three days earlier, back in Kansas, restated their wedding vows on the Sea of Galilee. People shared testimonies of their life in Christ and we concluded with hymns, singing in the drenching rain.

The pages of my Bible became rain-stained on that day. But they are still readable. They reveal the calming answer to all "storms." When tossed about on the sea of Galilee, Christ's disciples discovered that answer; it came in the form of a Person. Would that same Person calm my storm? How would my prayer, "Jehovah God, please show me the "real Truth," be answered?

Chapter 9
Honey, I Just Asked Jesus..."

"I once was lost, but now am found, was blind, but now I see." "How precious did that grace appear; the hour I first believed" "Amazing Grace" - John Newton

Jerusalem was in a heat wave. An Iranian high-pressure front had pushed the Holy City's temperature ten degrees above normal. It reached 96 degrees. During that June in 2007, Roselie and I were walking Jerusalem's Mount Zion area. I longed to descend the steep stone-paved path to the pool of Siloam. Taking refuge from the sun under a small shade tree, Roselie remained behind.

As I walked down the old path I thought of the blind man some two millennia earlier, poking his stick as he hobbled down the same pathway. Jesus had spat into the soil making clay, and he rubbed it onto the man's eyes. What had that blind man been thinking, perhaps on a hot day like this? Surely his hopes had been raised. He must have known he was in the presence of no ordinary man. Jesus ordered him, "Go wash in the pool of Siloam." I too wanted to wash my eyes in Siloam's pool at the bottom of the hill.

* * * *

In 1980, twenty-seven years before, this, my third Holy Land tour, that same teacher from Galilee was approaching me. Though I couldn't see him, I could sense I was in the presence of no ordinary man. He would invite me too to trust him, placing faith in him. My ailment? Spiritual blindness. How would he cure me?

As I worked in my photo darkroom I wondered, "How could I be doing this?" I was developing a new habit, listening to gospel music on radio.

As a teen, I once rebuked my father, "Dad you shouldn't be listening to that kind of music on the radio!" Dad was listening to an old hymn, "I Love to Tell the Story." "That hymn has its origin in false religion! Furthermore, it inappropriately glorifies Jesus," I complained. The offensive words were, "I love to tell the story of Jesus and his glory, of Jesus and his love."

At age twenty-three, as presiding overseer in the Franklinville, New York Congregation of Jehovah's Witnesses, a friend's husband had died suddenly. The friend and her daughter were Witnesses and the deceased was Baptist. Could I give the funeral talk? Yes. Would it be permissible to have a popular local singer come to the graveside to sing the man's favorite hymn? I hastily answered yes. But as the funeral date neared I became troubled about allowing a "false religious hymn."

Hours before the funeral I phoned the Watchtower Society's headquarters for advice. I knew it was permissible to preach a funeral for a non-Witness, unless he had once been a Witness and turned apostate. But what should I do about the songster coming to sing the deceased man's favorite hymn? The brother on the phone scolded: "You shouldn't have allowed the hymn! Now that you have, you must not go to the graveside, you must not be associated in any way with false religion, including its music."

I told the grieving wife and daughter I would give the funeral talk, but I would not accompany them to the graveside for the usual scripture reading and committal prayer. All our Jehovah's Witness friends followed my lead, avoiding the graveside service. The offensive hymn sung at the graveside service? "There'll be Peace in the Valley."

But now living in Virginia at age 33, I had begun an earnest search for the real truth. I had appealed to God. I believed with all my heart that he had heard my prayer. With the authoritarianism of Jehovah's Witnesses fading from my horizon, I felt drawn to gospel music. How did this transition happen?

My radio stayed tuned to Martinsville's WMVA. I enjoyed the station's local talk shows. Sunday mornings I sometimes continued my week's work, developing professional photographers' photos in my darkroom. Sunday morning radio programming was centered on gospel music and preaching services.

On Sundays, I began listening to music I never even knew existed, "Amazing Grace" and "How Great Thou Art" and other songs about Jesus. The words and tunes stirred something inside me, like those wonderful chills of delight I had sensed during the singing of "The Lord's Prayer."

I cannot explain the depth to which the songs penetrated my psyche. I recall just sitting there weeping and wondering. "What's wrong with me, I'm a grown man, I shouldn't be crying. What is it about this music?" I did not realize it at the time, but gospel music was the first phase in the answer to my prayer, "Jehovah God please show me the real truth."

The summer of 1980 brought the most violent weather in my memory. I had seldom been frightened by lightning and thunder. Previously I enjoyed it, and sometimes ventured outside to photograph nighttime lightning. One storm hung over our house and would not budge. Brilliant lightning flashed, and deafening thunder shook the windows for an eternity. I became frightened. I went onto the porch and, without forethought, nervously whispered out loud, "Jesus Christ help us." Immediately a peace came over me. Then I was struck by the thought, "I've never spoken directly to Jesus before." It had always been wrong to talk to Jesus, pray to him or worship him. The centerpiece of our Jehovah's Witness theology was: Jesus is not God; he's a created being, namely Michael the Archangel. You worship only Jehovah who is God the Father. Jesus was only "a god" according to John 1:1 in our own *New World Translation*. You must not worship Jesus because he is only a lesser god.

Six hundred miles away Mom was suffering a near mental breakdown. She had cared for her aging parents until their deaths at very old ages. She was worn-out physically and emotionally. Our family, now with four children, traveled north to visit. To console Mom, I shared my talking-to-Jesus-in-the-storm experience. Perhaps she could get relief from her stress as I had during the storm. I suggested she too talk to Jesus about her issues. Mom gave a mild rebuke, "Well, Dwight, we know Jesus is God's son and we're to pray in his name when we pray to his father Jehovah, but we never speak directly to Jesus. We talk only to Almighty God Jehovah." I was genuinely trying to help, but my suggestion only repulsed her. Mom's recovery was slow and never complete, I believe I compounded her anxiety. I'm sure she sensed the beginning of my falling away from the truth. I departed Mom, burdened for her wellbeing.

First, I had opened myself up to gospel music and now the second step, actually speaking to Jesus for the first time ever. The third and decisive step soon followed.

At 11:00 each Sunday morning the station broadcasted a live church service from the Horsepasture Christian Church. I was curious about the church's name. Far more intriguing, the church's pastor Ray Wells used the divine name, "Jehovah" in his sermons. "He can't be too amiss," I thought, "He's using God's name in his preaching." I tuned in week after week.

Each week, Pastor Wells preached from the Bible book of Isaiah. On August 3, 1980, he preached on Chapter 53. Sitting in my darkroom, enlarging photos, I was captivated by his sermon on "the suffering servant." Isaiah had described in painstaking detail the coming Messiah. As Wells expounded the scripture text, he explained how Jesus perfectly fulfilled the role of the promised Messiah. He had come not to rule from an earthly throne but to suffer as atonement for the sins of those who believe in Him. His sufferings were beyond human comprehension. His agony multiplied when those he loved most rejected him.

The Isaiah scripture verses took on celestial meaning to me as Pastor Wells recited the old prophet's inspired predictions:

He was despised and rejected by men,

a man of sorrows, and familiar with suffering.

Like one from whom men hide their faces

he was despised, and we esteemed him not.

Surely he took up our infirmities

and carried our sorrows,

yet we considered him stricken by God,

smitten by him, and afflicted.

But he was pierced for our transgressions,

he was crushed for our iniquities;

the punishment that brought us peace was upon him,

and by his wounds we are healed.

We all, like sheep, have gone astray,

each of us has turned to his own way;

and the LORD has laid on him

the iniquity of us all. Isaiah 53:3-6

The promised "suffering servant" clearly fit Jesus of Nazareth. Pastor Wells extolled the virtues of the Lord Jesus Christ, highlighting his sufferings and forgiveness while nailed to the cross. He personalized Christ's love. Jesus died for me because I had inherited by nature, sin and wretchedness.

How could this Jesus love me so deeply? Why would he willingly suffer and die for a world of sinners like me? Immediately I sensed unfathomable love. At last the stage was set for the most significant event of my entire life.

The Pastor concluded his message with this invitation, "If there's anyone here today without the Lord Jesus Christ, come." Without a second's hesitation, I prayed, "Lord Jesus I need you, please come into my heart, and forgive my sins." At once I felt an enormous weight lift off me. I felt light enough to soar like an eagle. At last I was free.

In a minute or so I came beaming through the darkroom door. Roselie was busy preparing lunch. I excitedly exclaimed "Honey, I just asked Jesus to come into my heart, and I feel so good!"

She glared back, "Does this mean you believe in the Trinity?"

Undaunted I replied, "I don't know. All I know is, I have peace inside me like I've never had before."

She said no more but I saw on her countenance fear and confusion.

My prayer of six months earlier was answered. As it turned out the, real Truth was not a religious organization after all. The real Truth was a person. Jesus answered, 'I am the way and the truth and the life. No one comes to my Father except through me'" (John 14:6).

Jesus was a person with the power to forgive my transgressions; a person with the desire and authority to grant me an eternal heavenly future with him. He was a person who had all along coveted a relationship with me. "Come to me, all you who are weary and burdened, and I will give you rest... for I am gentle and humble in heart, and you will find rest for your souls. For my yoke is easy and my burden is light" (Matthew11:28-30).

Like a prisoner released from a dungeon, everything looked bright, new and clean. My pardon had come at great cost to Jesus, my newly discovered Savior.

* * * *

Twenty-seven years later I literally washed my eyes in Jerusalem's Pool of Siloam. There at the pool, wiping the water from my eyes I went back to that August 1980 day and the moment when, like the formerly blind man, I could say, "I was blind but now I see!" Like the newly healed blind man there would be a personal cost, how would other Witnesses react to my exciting new experience? Such concerns barely entered my mind, my sins were forgiven, the Truth had set me free!

Chapter 10
On Trial

"But when they deliver you up, take no thought how or what ye shall speak: for it shall be given you in that same hour what ye shall speak. For it is not ye that speak, but the Spirit of your Father which speaketh in you." Matthew 10:19,20 KJV

I walked up the long hill from Siloam's pool, in the age-old footsteps of a newly healed blind man. He was blind from birth and had trodden the same path home. His family and friends were astounded. But word of such a miracle could not be hidden around Jerusalem. Soon the authoritarian Pharisees summoned the blind man. They must investigate the man's claims. Was his healing genuine? Who was responsible for performing this miracle? Thus, working on the Sabbath and violating their Sabbath rules?

Would the guilty party be Jesus of Nazareth? He had already caused much trouble for the authorities. The crowd was becoming more interested in this rabbi, Jesus, than in their own religious leaders. Did not everyone know that the Jewish religious authorities had already decided to put out of the synagogue, ostracizing and stripping of ordinary civil rights, anyone who acknowledged that Yeshua Ha Maschia, Jesus is Messiah.

Back to 1980. Roselie was still attending the Witness meetings. Her sister faithfully chauffeured her and our four children to the Kingdom Hall. My wife later admitted that she could only hope and pray that I would return to "the truth," that my "feeling" would soon pass, restoring normal life again. News travels fast amongst the Witness community. They soon learned of my "falling away." Rather than facing the reality of my defection, the brothers made excuses for my "aberrant" thinking. Several elders admonished, "Dwight, you've been through a lot; you may need some time to think." I wasn't looking for sympathy. It seemed incomprehensible to my friends that something extraordinary, something supernatural had changed my life.

A Witness elder, whom I greatly respected, tried to restore me. He recalled his own experience from several years earlier. Before he became a Jehovah's Witness, he too had responded to an invitation to "come to Jesus." He "walked the aisle" in a local church; he prayed, and he had gotten a good feeling. "I got saved, born again, but the feeling was gone within six months," he said. "Dwight this feeling you have; it will only last six months. I found that only Jehovah's Witnesses have the truth."

Contrary to his prognostication, the "feeling" indeed persisted. In fact, the word "feeling" minimizes the deep reality of my metamorphosis. So much was changing. I no longer depended on my old friend Jack Daniels, instead, I saw God as a personal friend; a companion who lifted my spirits. God wasn't angry and demanding after all. He was caring and patient, willing to put up with me. He loved me beyond comprehension. He had forgiven all my sins.

I no longer tried to dismiss Jesus' claims to Deity. From the Bible, I could see that Jesus was Almighty God in the flesh. Jesus is Jehovah God just as Christians have believed throughout church history. Yes! I soon believed in the Holy Trinity. I knew the bliss of being filled with the Holy Spirit as well as having the

Father and Son's indwelling just as Jesus promised (see John 14:15-17, 23).

I felt the joy of being liberated from authoritarian religion with its impossible burden of manmade rules.

The brothers were obligated to prepare for my hearing, they must follow organizational protocol, urging me to repent, returning to God's "ark," the Watchtower organization. Unless I recanted and denied my conversion to the Lord Christ, they must disfellowship me. "Why would I ever want to go back?" I thought, "I've been forgiven, even if I had wanted to go back, how could I become unforgiven again?" Absurd! Jesus, by his blood, had washed away my sins, how could a person become unforgiven again?

Roselie vacillated from "I think I'll divorce you, you apostate!" to "I think I'll read the Bible without the Watchtower literature. I will prove from the Bible alone; Jesus is not God." Our spiritual conversations were few. I felt that any significant change in her viewpoint would have to come directly from God and without much input from me. When she seemed closed to discussion, I retreated to my photo darkroom and prayed, "Lord Jesus please show my wife the real Truth.

As the weeks passed I observed a softening. Still she swung back and forth, one day leaning toward Watchtower dogma, the next wondering if they could be in error. But for the first time she seemed to question the Society's teaching. "Just maybe Jesus could be God," she said. The struggle, as always, centered on "Who is Jesus?"

Sensing her precarious spiritual dilemma, one Witness elder even suggested the possibility of divorce. That disturbing prospect brought tears to Roselie's eyes as she shared how much she loved me and would never want our family to be divided. But, I could easily mislead her into "false doctrines," she was told. Would she remain loyal to the organization? Or would God answer my prayer, revealing Jesus as the real Truth?

A neighbor man repeated his psychologist brother's observation, our marriage would likely fail. I believe such negative suggestions helped to convince Roselie, come hell or high water, she would stay in her marriage.

I discovered Christian radio, first WWMO in Reidsville, North Carolina and then WRVL in Lynchburg, Virginia. I listened intently as I processed photos. The stations filled my day with Christian music and scholarly Bible teaching.

I soon felt the need to fellowship with other Christians. Which church should I attend? Through a neighbor, I had met a Christian couple, Alfred and Dorothy Hurt who seemed earnest in their faith. I decided to attend their church, Western Light Tabernacle in Moneta, VA. Preacher Clayton Leonard welcomed me that first Sunday night. I was immediately surrounded by a band of loving, caring Christians. Their opening song was "Tis so Sweet to Trust in Jesus." Now at last I was in a church to worship, not just taking pictures.

At this point, I was going to church and Roselie was still going to the Kingdom Hall. Roselie and I sat down with our elder children Karrie (age 12) and Doug (age 9). We asked them who they would like to go with on Sundays. They, without hesitation, replied, "We'll go to church with dad!" I was taken by surprise and Roselie was stunned. The younger children, Billy (age 3) and Amy (age 1) accompanied Roselie to the Kingdom Hall.

The older children's choice of church naturally changed their school life. Doug had a Witness classmate. He tried not to embarrass his buddy as he shed Witnesses rules. He and his friend had supported each other in refusing to participate in forbidden patriotic and holiday activities. I now allowed Karrie and Doug to join in singing formerly forbidden songs. They could now pledge allegiance to the flag, although they had to first learn the words. They participated in the Thanksgiving play and Christmas program.

After school Karrie and Doug would go to "Gilligan's Island," their secret play area in the woods, a flowing stream divided to create an "island." Doug strummed his guitar, the two children sang over and over, the first and only verse they knew of "The Old Rugged Cross ":

On a hill far away stood an old rugged cross,

The emblem of suffering and shame;

And I love that old cross where the dearest and best

For a world of lost sinners was slain.

So I'll cherish the old rugged cross

Till my trophies at last I lay down;

I will cling to the old rugged cross,

And exchange it someday for a crown.

My children were singing, making a joyful noise. The cross which we had so despised, now had a wondrous attraction to us.

Amidst the wonders of a new life, filled with both struggles and great joys, I received "the letter," a letter informing me of my committee hearing. Should I even attend such an inquiry?

Yes! Four years earlier Gary and Judy's attendance at their committee hearing had impacted my life. Would the Lord somehow use my words? Could I help sway someone? Perhaps one of the elders or even my wife?

In a role reversal, I the former committee inquisitor would now become the interrogated. How would I answer the committee's questions?

The committee invited me to explain rumors they had heard about me, could I meet with them at the Kingdom Hall on October 31, 1980? Their intention was to determine my thoughts about these essential theological questions: Who is Jesus? Do you now believe Jesus is God? Do you believe in the Trinity? Are you telling people you are "born again?"

As a loyal wife, Roselie decided to attend with me. We arranged for her mom to watch our kids during the committee hearing. While Roselie and her mother conversed nervously in her mom's kitchen, I knelt on the tiled bathroom floor and prayed silently, "Lord Jesus, please give me the right words for tonight." I was keenly aware of my inability to defend doctrines I had only a short time ago despised.

The Rocky Mount Judicial Committee, as expected, tried to reason with me, asking me to explain my new beliefs. They gently pointed out my "error." They used the customary Witness reasoning, trying to disprove my newly embraced "false" doctrines.

A new Christian for less than four months, with minimal doctrinal understanding, I recited my story. I had prayed for the truth to be revealed. I knew that "God so loved the world, that he gave his only begotten Son, that whosoever believeth in him should not perish, but have everlasting life." (see John 3:16). Believing in Christ for salvation was the same doctrine held by Christians for centuries, I explained. The theologically technical questions followed. My wife was dumbfounded by my clear answers. She couldn't understand, how was I able to answer the brothers? The committee likewise appeared astonished. They wondered from where I had gotten these teachings; later asking Roselie if I was studying materials from Billy Graham or perhaps Jerry Falwell? How had I fallen so far from the truth?

No one was more surprised than me! From where was my powerful Biblical defense coming? How could I explain the established tenets of Christianity? I had listened for a few weeks to Christian radio shows. But my many years of Watchtower studies were always belittling church doctrines. My only answer, my Lord heard the bathroom prayer. He stood near me and infused me with the power of his Holy Spirit.

A week passed after our Halloween night meeting with the committee. Following the regular Thursday night Kingdom Hall meeting, Roselie entered our home with red, tear-filled eyes. I held her tightly in my arms. She sobbed, "They read the notice tonight; you're disfellowshipped for 'conduct unbecoming a Christian.' It would be easier to die than to go through this."

Complicating matters, that same Thursday night, the committee coincidentally disfellowshipped another Witness. A woman for "conduct unbecoming a Christian." The Society always instructed each

Congregation to use nonspecific terminology to reduce the possibility of libel suits against the Witnesses. Roselie feared that some at the Kingdom Hall would surmise an immoral connection between the woman and me, even though the reasons were entirely unrelated, and the woman was unknown to us. It was an awkward situation. So, I decided to go public. I wrote a letter to the editor of The Roanoke Times explaining my situation. I had been disfellowshipped for confessing Jesus as my Lord and my God. The Times sent a writer who wrote a lengthy account of my story.

On Christmas morning 1980, I fetched the newspaper. There on the front page, under the huge headline BANISHED, was my picture with children, Karrie and Doug as we stood singing "Jesus Loves Me" with a Christian hymnal in our hands. The article was well-researched, accurate, and written fairly. All our Witness friends could now see there was no connection between the other disfellowshipped person and myself. However, I am sure our Witness friends were dismayed, even enraged, reading a "tell all" story of a former Witness leader who left "the truth" having found a better way, Jesus.

At first, I thought the article presented me in an ungracious light, perhaps painting me as angry at the Witnesses. Through the years, I have become more gracious and empathetic towards Jehovah's Witnesses individually. However, I am less sympathetic toward their authoritarian leaders. I wish for a reformation amongst the Witnesses. I pray that they will corporately reject their leaders' notions and adopt the teachings of Christianity.

That same week, a church friend was called on by Jehovah's Witnesses. My friend, referring to the front-page article, told the Witness, "I'm a friend of

Dwight Hayes." The Witness man snorted angrily, "I bet they're paying him a lot of money to say those lies." I too once had a persecution-complex. I believed our enemies would say anything to defame our religious authority, the Watchtower Society.

The front-page article was almost too much for Roselie to suffer. She did not leave the house for more than a week. She is private and resists publicity of any kind. But in just a few days something incredible began to happen.

The newspaper article spoke of Roselie's continued loyalty to the Watchtower organization; it was distributed on the Associated Press. Christians of all denominations and from diverse addresses bombarded us with cards. There were Christmas cards, "thinking of you" cards, and letters. Dozens of well-wishers urged me to hang in there with Jesus. The cards exuded love and concern for beleaguered Roselie. As we unsealed each envelope we sensed love and genuine concern from the Christian community.

"We are so glad to hear of your decision; may God bless you." "We're praying for you and Roselie." "We love you." "We're struggling with a family member who's interested in Jehovah's Witnesses; thank you for your willingness to be candid about these people." The letters continued.

Roselie was deeply moved. No Witnesses had written to encourage her to stay with the truth. She later received a starkly worded letter from a Witness known to us, the writer urged her to stand faithfully in opposition to her husband's new faith. It was joyless and discouraging.

Roselie began her search for truth. She clandestinely attended church with me. She understood the cost if she were found out. She was warmly received at the Tabernacle. Church women prayed for her and lovingly reached out to her.

Meanwhile, I wondered what had happened to Gary and Judy. Perhaps Judy with her sweet spirit that had so convicted me could help Roselie, being former Witnesses, they would understand our situation. The committee and I had dis-fellowshipped them some four years earlier for the same "crime" for which I was now banished. Amazingly, we obtained their address from a Christian bookstore operator back in the state of New York. They had moved twice first to Utica, New York and from there to Atlanta. I was given their current address. If I were to phone them, how would I be received? I had fractured their family by disfellowshipping them for apostasy. But now I too was born-again, would they be angry because of the unspeakable hurt I had caused them? Would Judy agree to help Roselie?

* * * *

Back to the Holy City, Jerusalem. Roselie and I sought refuge from the midday sun, sitting beneath a eucalyptus tree on the Temple Mount. Likely the no longer blind man had been summoned near here to stand trial before an angry party of religious authorities. He remained bold in his witness. His healer was the man "they called Jesus." The trial went against him; Pharisees "put him out" of the synagogue. He was banished for acknowledging that his healer, Jesus, was from God.

A few moments later Jesus found the dishonored man. He asked him, "Do you believe in the Son of Man?" Jesus identified himself. The dishonored man believed, receiving forgiveness of his sins; he worshipped Jesus right here, in this vicinity. The former blind man departed a scorned man, but what did it matter? For as he confessed "I was blind but now I see!" (see John 9).

Chapter 11
I Have Decided to Follow Jesus

"...Where you go, I will go, and where you stay I will stay. Your people will be my people, and your God my God." Ruth 1:16

An Arab family was harvesting olives. A man violently shook its branches. Children in its limbs beat off stubborn fruit. Like a hail storm, olives rained onto a spread-out sheet, collecting the tree's harvest. A woman sitting on the ground plucked off stems and bagged the crop, carrying the produce to a waiting car. I was standing on a ridge looking south towards the town of Bethlehem.

As I surveyed the hilly scene beyond the immediate olive grove, I thought of the multitude of heaven's angels praising God and saying, "Glory to God in the highest..." And I pictured the humble shepherds saying, "Let us go to Bethlehem and see this thing that has happened."

I also envisioned the boy David, an ancestor of Jesus, shepherding his father Jesse's flock. Suddenly a lion attacked a lamb. The youth ran towards the attacker, rescuing the lamb. David grabbed the lion by its mane and killed the animal with his hands. Another time he killed a bear caught attacking his sheep.

I pictured David's great-grandmother Ruth, a young widow, walking arm-in-arm with mother-in-law Naomi. Perhaps that winding lane now stretching before my eyes is actually where the two women walked and talked. Ruth declared her loyalty to her Israelite mother-in-law and her loyalty to the God of Naomi's family, the God of Israel.

Ruth's devotion to Naomi and to her God reminded me of Roselie's loyalty to me and my God. But there was a time when my wife was still searching for the God I had just come to know. Who would help her in her search? In 1980, I asked for help from the very ones I had banished from Jehovah's Witnesses.

My heart pounded as I dialed the Atlanta number.

"Hello," a man answered.

"Hi, is this Gary?"

"Yes, it is."

"This is Dwight Hayes, I'm one of the Elders who disfellowshipped you and Judy."

A long pause, "Yes, I remember you."

"Gary I'm a Christian now, I am so sorry for what I did to you and your family."

(Indistinct conversation in the background)

"I'm going to put Judy on the phone too."

I continued, "Judy I'm really sorry for my part in disfellowshipping you and splitting your family."

"Dwight! I'm so glad you're saved!" Judy was jubilant. She exclaimed,

"Welcome to the family of God!"

I breathed a sigh of relief, they eagerly inquired about my conversion. It is rare for a Jehovah's Witness to convert to Christ; I have noticed that many ex-Witnesses seem to slowly drift away from all religious affiliation. For me to become a follower of Jesus, that was reason for Judy's jubilation.

"Judy," I continued, "Would you speak to Roselie? She has questions about the Trinity and other doctrines." Roselie had consented to talk with Judy, knowing the severe consequences if the elders discovered any communication with a disfellowshipped person. Roselie was permitted to talk to me as her husband, but not about spiritual things, a rule she sometimes found hard to obey.

Roselie found comfort in talking to Judy. Roselie realized that Judy knew the "Witness language," and Judy could understand and answer her questions with relevance. In Judy's four years as a Christian, she had diligently researched the scriptures. In ensuing phone conversations Judy's kindly manner and answers from the Bible caused Roselie to reflect, Jesus might be the Way, He could be God in the flesh.

In December 1980, we visited Gary and Judy in Atlanta. We were warmly received. They introduced us to other ex-Jehovah's Witnesses. Among those were Helen Ortega and her daughter Debbie. They had been Witnesses for twenty years prior to being disfellowshipped for becoming Christians. With motherlike encouragement Helen urged Roselie to seek Jesus with all her heart, she promised to earnestly pray for her, Helen wrote and phoned to support her.

In Atlanta, we also met a young Bible college graduate named David Henke. He had just launched a counter-cult ministry called Watchman Fellowship. Henke's focus centered on identifying religious cults and providing a Christian response to their teachings.

David's in-depth research on the Watchtower Society appalled us. So many Witness beliefs, like a pendulum, had swung back and forth, first introducing a new doctrine, then reversing it, and then back to their original understanding once again. The Watchtower Society's teachings on the Lordship of Christ however did not flip flop as did many of their other doctrines. They progressively distanced themselves from the Lordship of Christ. (see discussion on the Lordship of Christ in the appendix, pgs. 177, 178)

A few months later in the spring 1981, Gary and Judy with their two children would visit us in Virginia. Those few days would prove a blessing.

By January 1981, Roselie had concluded from scripture that Jesus is the only Way. The folks at the Tabernacle and the ex-Witnesses from the Atlanta area were patiently praying for the Lord to bring my wife to the ultimate decision, that of "believing in the Lord Jesus Christ as Savior."

I recall Roselie exclaiming. "I did ask Jesus to come into my heart, but nothing happened, I expected a similar experience to yours." I didn't know how to respond to her. But I did see changes in her thinking. She attended her last Witness meeting. Her thoughts were almost identical to mine at my last meeting. "I don't belong here! I don't believe these things anymore!" She had that same fish-out-of-the water feeling, like struggling in a hostile environment. She had become more comfortable attending church and singing songs such as "Amazing Grace" or "When I Survey the Cross."

Roselie's mother, Carrie, had been associated with the Witnesses for thirty years. She raised her daughters to be faithful Jehovah's Witnesses. She also relocated to Virginia a year or so after our move. She longed to be near our family. Of Carrie's nine children, I believe Roselie and she were closest. Naturally Carrie was concerned for her daughter's spirituality because of my disfellowshipping. Her concern increased as time passed; Roselie stopped door-to-door witnessing and no longer attended meetings.

Roselie waited for the uncomfortable opportunity to inform her mom; she had decided to leave the Witnesses to follow Jesus. Roselie realized that this would likely be their last farewell. Witness elders would force Carrie to no longer fellowship with her daughter. On each visit, Roselie tried to bring up the difficult subject; but it just wasn't the right time to talk about it. Then one chilly March afternoon, Carrie herself approached the subject. "Roselie, you said you have questions about the organization?" Previously Roselie had expressed her concerns about several troubling Witness practices, such as "counting time." All Jehovah's Witnesses were required to report monthly the number of hours spent in house-to-house activity. It troubled Roselie that one's spiritual condition was often evaluated by the quantity of hours spent in field service and the amount of literature placed with householders.

Another example, Roselie had been conflicted over the Watchtower Society's refusal to let Jehovah's Witnesses observe Mother's Day. The Witness logic being the celebration must be avoided because it honors a human parent rather than God. Yet one of the Bible's Ten Commandments decree "Honor your Father and Mother." (see pgs. 192-193)

But most troubling of all was the Watchtower Society's condescending view of the Lordship of Jesus. Roselie responded to her mother's inquiry. I believe she spoke with God-given strength, uttering words beyond human ability, verbalizing the most difficult words of her life. "Ma I'm not going back to the Kingdom Hall, I love Jesus more than the Watchtower organization. I know they're not going to let us talk anymore. I want you to know I love you, but I love Jesus even more." They wept.

Roselie sobbed, "The Witnesses will try to tell you that I've been pressured into leaving the organization, being wrongly swayed by new "worldly" friends. But no one has coerced me. This is my own decision; I have decided to follow Jesus."

Then through tears, Carrie assured her that Jesus would give her friends, replacing those "friends" who would be forced to shun her for Jesus sake.

My mother-in-law's prophetic words were already being fulfilled, dozens of Christian well-wishers had mailed encouraging Christmas letters, our new Tabernacle acquaintances accepted us as kinfolk, and ex-Witness Christians in Atlanta were befriending us.

Still, I puzzled over Carrie's parting words. She had spoken as if she knew Jesus. No Witness would speak about Jesus' personal care for us. Her comment personalizing Jesus' love would not be forthcoming from a Jehovah's Witness. Somewhere in Carrie's past there must have been an encounter with Christ's love, some secret memory of meeting Jesus, hidden away from decades ago.

* * * *

Izzy, our Israeli guide, interrupted my thoughts returning me to the present. He beckoned, "Time to board the bus for Jerusalem."

Like Ruth's oath of loyalty sworn to Naomi, here in the hills stretching before me, Roselie too had chosen to follow my lead, fellowshipping with new friends, giving allegiance to my God and Naomi's God, the God of Israel, the God of Christianity.

Chapter 12
Roselie Faces the Elders

"Though my father and mother forsake me, the LORD will receive me." Psalms 27:10

A sad young man wept near Jerusalem's Garden tomb. I asked him if he needed to talk to someone.

"Yes", he answered, "I'm from England, my wife and I attended an evangelical church there. Recently a traveling evangelist spoke at our church. He said that God didn't use Mary's egg in the conception of Jesus, but rather God implanted a supernatural egg in her womb for the conception of Jesus."

I said, "That doesn't sound right to me, it sounds like an ancient heresy that denies the full humanity of Christ."

"Yes, that's what I thought too. I went to the church elders, but they wouldn't hear me. In fact, they accused me of causing disunity in the church because I questioned the evangelist's teaching. They asked me to leave the church. We have family members in the church, I love my church. I'm broken-hearted."

I reflected on my experience, being banished from my long-held faith. The religion of my family and friends. Had God brought this man and me together at this holy place, so I could comfort him, a dispirited Christian? What could I say to him? Twenty-five years earlier my wife had faced Witness elders with different charges but still centering around the person of Christ.

Roselie had trusted Christ as her Savior. She accepted the orthodox view of Jesus as God. She sent a letter of resignation to the elders. Would they accept her voluntary departure from the Watchtower organization? Or would they find it necessary to punish her for her private thoughts and personal beliefs? They instructed her to meet with the committee at the Rocky Mount Kingdom Hall.

We agreed to meet with the elders. Refusing to appear would have been less stressful. We felt the outcome was fairly certain. Still we hoped something Roselie might say would have a lasting influence on the elders. Maybe they too would someday see Christ as the Truth instead of a human organization. We prayed that their eyes might be opened.

For moral support, I accompanied Roselie to the Rocky Mount Kingdom Hall. The chairman asked her,

"Who is Jesus?"

She quoted John 14:6: "Jesus answered, 'I am the way and the truth and the life.'"

"I believe Jesus is the Truth," she said.

The elder continued "**Where** will you go?" As if there was no truth or life outside the Witnesses.[10]

"It's not **where** I'm going, but it's to **whom**, I'm going," she answered. "I'm going to a person, Jesus Christ, not to just another religious organization."

---

[10] As a former elder in the Witness, I also had often misquoted Peter's words. Actually, Peter asked "...Lord, to <u>whom</u> shall we go? You have the sayings of eternal life" (see John 6:68 – underlined for emphasis)

"Do you now believe in the Trinity?" they continued.

"The Bible says, 'The Word [Jesus] was with God and the Word [Jesus] was God.'" (see John 1:1,14)

"I believe Jesus is God." The questions continued. I sometimes intervened with comments. The elders found my responses objectionable, they found me offensive, I was sharply rebuked.

"We are here to talk to your wife, not you," the chairman retorted. I discovered that Roselie was giving powerful answers without my help, God was her Protector.

A few days after the meeting we received the letter. We were informed that the committee found Roselie guilty of "conduct unbecoming a Christian." They had disfellowshipped her. Roselie was at peace with the outcome. At my disfellowshipping she had grieved and suffered through the firestorm with immeasurable pain. She seemed to be a different person now, more serene, more joyful and more positive, as if freed of a heavy load. There was no evidence that any of the committee elders were influenced by her testimony about Jesus.

Jehovah's Witnesses do not allow a woman to pray in the presence of her husband. Married twelve years and religiously devout, Roselie had never prayed audibly in my presence. Now for the first time we prayed together. My heart was deeply moved. Her prayers were sincere and powerful.

Shunning a disfellowshipped child wasn't new to Carrie, Roselie's mother. She had already suffered the pain of Witness-ordered shunning for more than a dozen years.

Carrie, a widow, had struggled alone, attempting to raise six sons and three daughters as a dedicated Jehovah's Witnesses. Three of her sons, Roselie and the twin sisters were baptized, indicating acceptance of all Watchtower teachings. Eventually two sons were disfellowshipped; Douglas for joining a Baptist church and Tom for smoking cigarettes. Now Roselie was disfellowshipped for recognizing Christ as her Lord and God. All three children had committed "sins" forbidden by the Watchtower Society.

Three of Carrie's children remained loyal to the Witnesses, three made no religious claims, and three had broken their mother's heart, bringing scorn on the Witnesses, "falling away" from "the truth" resulting in disfellowshipping. Carrie must now shun her dearest earthly friend, her beloved daughter, Roselie.[11]

Back in the mid 1970's, I once hid in Ma's bathroom because her disfellowshipped son Douglas brought his family to visit Roselie's mother. Ma and Roselie ignored Douglas. They focused their conversation on his wife and children. I waited, perched on the commode for an hour, until they left. Speaking to him would be wrong, disobeying God's organization, subjecting myself to discipline, and displeasing to God. I was determined to obey God. Fortunately, no one needed to go during their visit.

---

[11] *Disfellowshipping rules have changed from time to time. Generally, people within the same household were permitted to speak to a disfellowshipped family member. They must not discuss spiritual subjects. Extended families were not allowed to speak to a disfellowshipped family member, except to discuss legal or health issues. For example, an elderly parent's health and care.*

Shortly after my 1980 disfellowshipping and six months before Roselie's acceptance of Christ, I phoned her Christian brother Douglas and told him I had met Jesus. I requested his forgiveness for shunning him for a dozen years. He was elated with the news. He assured me of his friendship and promised to pray for his sister Roselie. He asked his daughter Laurie Ann to send us her gospel music. She was traveling with a Christian singing troupe. Her singing touched our hearts.

In the months leading up to Roselie's commitment to Christ, estranged members of her natural family were praying for her, lovingly reaching out, offering their friendship.

My darkroom prayer of six months earlier, "Jesus please show Roselie the real Truth, had been answered. Now we rejoined her disfellowshipped family as disfellowshipped Christians. Her brother Tom likewise professed Christ as Lord. He and his family joined our growing circle of friends.

As Jehovah's Witnesses, we had isolated ourselves from most non-Witnesses, including relatives. Now we sought fellowship and reconnected with three more of Roselie's non-Witness brothers and their families. As relationships warmed, family friends numbered in the dozens. Our children became acquainted, for the first time, with aunts, uncles and cousins on my wife's side of the family.

Carrie's paradoxical words, "Jesus will give you friends," still puzzled me. Jehovah's Witnesses never said anything about a personal relationship with Jesus Christ, but Carrie had spoken as if she knew Jesus and trusted him as a close friend. Her prophetic words saw a flood of fulfillment. We began to reunite with blood relatives, a multitude of them, and many were likewise believers in Jesus. But Ma remained obedient to the Watchtower Society's disfellowshipping rule. She shunned Roselie. Since our children had not been baptized as Witnesses, they were not liable for their parents' "sins." They were innocent, so Witnesses could speak to them if they desired. Roselie and I arranged to drop our kids off at her mom's apartment and pick them up again at a prearranged time. The visits were cordial. Carrie didn't try to convert them. This way her Mom could obey the organization and still see her grandchildren without facing Roselie or me.

A few times Roselie and her mom did come face-to-face in public. My wife described one unplanned meeting at the grocery store. Carrie acted nervous, limited her conversation to trivial chit chat, and appeared fearful, as if a Witness elder was watching, listening, ready to report to the committee.

Carrie lived into her mid-eighties. In her later years, the Witness elders allowed us to temporarily care for her. Perhaps they reasoned Carrie, now troubled with dementia, was beyond being misled by "apostates" like Roselie and me. At this late stage in her life she seemed unaware of the rules forbidding spiritual conversations with disfellowshipped family members.

Ma had not celebrated Christmas for forty-five years. But in 1996 she enjoyed herself with our family. We sang Christmas carols, gave gifts, ate dinner, prayed together, took her to our church's Christmas cantata. Our church family loved her; they hugged and kissed her.

Once during that same year, while we cared for Ma in our place of business, a hospital chaplain friend of ours inquired of her,

"Carrie, do you know that Jesus loves you?"

Emphatically she answered, "Yes, when I was twelve years old I knew Jesus loved me!"

These were not the typical words of a Jehovah's Witness. At age twelve Carrie lived in a Methodist orphanage, in Randolph, New York. Had she discovered Christ's love many years ago, having trusted Jesus as a preteen, knowing the Jesus of Christianity all along, being a secret disciple like Joseph of Arimathea (see John 19:38), being afraid to confess the real Jesus lest she be "cast out" from the Witnesses and her circle of friends? (see John 9:22,23)

* * * *

Sitting near Jerusalem's Garden Tomb (June 2006) I was convinced that God had brought a troubled young man and me together so I could give him an encouraging word. I shared a brief testimony of my disfellowshipping. I told him of the comfort I found in Psalm 27:10, "Though my mother and father forsake me, the LORD will receive me." I prayed with him. I urged him to find a fellowship of Christians who rejected the heresy his church had embraced. Minutes later I had to leave with our group. I'd given him the only gift I could, encouragement from God's word. He appeared heartened and thanked me.

I departed the holy site in awe. Only God in his providence could have so precisely arranged our meeting. What a blessing to feel his presence in the likely place where Jesus had been raised from the tomb! What a joy to personally know God, the One who had strengthened my wife in her trial before the elders. The God who gave her strength to face the heartbreaking dilemma, being shunned by her mother!

Chapter 13
Farewell to Family/Family a Hundredfold

"'I tell you the truth,' Jesus replied, 'no one who has left home or brothers or sisters or mother or father or children or fields for me and the gospel will fail to receive a hundred times [hundredfold - KJV] as much in this present age (homes, brothers, sisters, mothers, children and fields–and with them, persecutions) and in the age to come, eternal life.'"

Mark 10:29,30

    Moses may have led the wandering Israelites into this extinct volcano, Petra. His brother Aaron is buried here. A spring flows from a split-in-two rock. Local Arabs call the spring Ain Musa meaning, "The Spring of Moses."

    November 2010 again found me in Petra, Jordan. Thousands of tourists were on hand beholding the amazing red sandstone hand-chiseled cityscape. I proceeded to the "Treasury of the Pharaoh" façade, wandering into a group of Irish-sounding folks. I asked where they were from. They were on a Christian tour from Britain and Ireland. I told them my relatives had come from Northern Ireland in the 1860's. My ancestors were Orangemen, Protestant Irish, loyal to the Queen. I shared an old family tale. On St. Patrick's Day, the boisterous men folk would crash pubs looking for Catholics to beat up. We laughed and joked, I felt a sense of kinship.

On a more serious note, I told them, "Actually I grew up neither Catholic nor Protestant. I was raised a Jehovah's Witness, becoming a local leader in that organization, I'm now a Christian, meeting Jesus thirty years ago. I was disfellowshipped from the Witnesses for professing Jesus as my Lord and my God. I lost more than fifty family members, but Jesus promised he would give me a hundredfold of 'brothers and sisters,' so whether you like me or not, you are my brothers and sisters!"

The group responded, almost in unison. "We love you."

I was asked, "Would you permit us to videotape five minutes of your testimony?" While we moved to a quieter area, I wondered what I would say in just five minutes.

As with these Irish and English Christians, I have been befriended by spiritual brothers and sisters a hundredfold, just as Jesus promised. But as for my extended family, of those who are Jehovah's Witnesses, I've seen every connection vanish. My last memories of those family relationships are described here.

My mom, Vera, was emotionally spent, night and day single-handedly caring for her parents, meeting their needs for years, until their dying day. I knew this would be a difficult time for Mom to learn of my life-changing decision. Word of my disfellowshipping reached her and Dad in a few days. I did not want to contribute to Mom's emotional stress, but neither could I live my life just to please her. I must follow the One who "first loved me" and forgave all my sins (see 1 John 4:19).

Mom had expressed her concern before my Jesus experience. She phoned, urging me not to miss the five

Witness meetings each week. She seemed worried that I might be drifting from the truth, questioning the Watchtower organization, slipping into apostasy. The worst fear for Jehovah's Witnesses is the news of their own child being disfellowshipped. It would be better if the defecting child had died.

Mom and I had been soul mates my entire life. We shared similar interests, dreaming imaginative dreams, inclined to creativity and not afraid to take risks. We faithfully followed Watchtower Society teaching.

Mom had once encouraged me to consider a career as a surgeon, performing surgeries without blood transfusions on fellow Jehovah's Witnesses. Back then few surgeons were willing to accept us as patients because they claimed the risk was too great. We refused all blood transfusions because the Bible in Leviticus Chapter 17 forbids eating blood. The Society quoted doctors who claimed that blood transfusions nourished the body similarly as does eating food. Therefore transfusions, according to the Witnesses, are the same as eating blood which is forbidden in the Bible.

Our unflagging obedience to "God's channel" the Watchtower organization meant we were willing to die if necessary. We would sign a liability waiver, but few doctors would take the risk, claiming their hands might be tied if they were to eliminate the life-saving possibility of transfusion. In refusing to accept as a patient a twelve-year-old with tonsillitis for whom I was advocating, one surgeon told me, "I've never needed to administer a blood transfusion for a tonsillectomy, but if my patient needs one, I will." When minor children of Jehovah's Witnesses faced a life-or-death medical crisis, courts often intervened, removing the child from parental custody and forcing a transfusion.

While committed to all Witness causes, I was not interested in medical work. Mom vastly overestimated my potential, urging me to consider surgery as a career.

I am sure Mom hoped I would be an exemplary Jehovah's Witness, a patriarch-like leader, encouraging family and friends to persevere in the truth. Surely Mom's confidence arose from my serious devotion to Watchtower doctrine.

I had been an early bloomer in the Witnesses, giving hour-long Sunday lectures at age 18; pioneering in full time house-to-house ministry. I was a congregation overseer (pastor) at age 23. I was handling speaking assignments on convention programs.

After our 1977 move to Virginia, nearly 600 miles separated our children from Mom and Dad. Our children, their first grandchildren, were far away, limiting fellowship and grandparent nurturing. We did travel to visit a few times each year. They visited us sometimes on their way south for the winter. For the next three years (1977-1980), Mom seemed to be losing her influence over me and my children.

Though forbidden by Jehovah's Witnesses' rules, Mom and I had a few discussions after my 1980 disfellowshipping. She tried restoring me to "the truth". Our conversation usually centered around the topic of sin.

As a Christian, I now identified with 18th century hymn writer, John Newton and first century Apostle Paul. In his legendary hymn "Amazing Grace," the former slave trader wrote, "Amazing grace, how sweet the sound that saved a wretch like me." Newton had engaged in the evils of slave trading; I had engaged in the destruction of families who professed Christ. Paul, formerly a persecutor of Christians, spoke of his daily struggle with sin, "What a wretched man I am! Who will rescue me from this body of death. Thanks be to God through Jesus Christ our Lord!" (Romans 7:24,25a)

I said, "Mom, what a wretch I've been. Jesus Christ, my Lord, forgave my sins, he saved me and forgave me. He's my best friend. Because I know and love him I want to spend eternity with him. I still love you Mom. I will always be willing to speak to you even though the elders forbid your speaking to me."

"Dwight, I raised my children to be good. You're not as wretched as you think," Mom countered.

From childhood, I had seen myself as hopeless and unworthy of entrance into the New World paradise preached by the Witnesses. My wife expressed similar feelings. Pleasing the God of the Watchtower was simply beyond our ability. He required more than we could ever give. Roselie and I were wearied and burdened by Watchtower doctrine, but now our burdens were lifted (see Matthew 11:28-30). We had accepted Jesus' invitation to "come to me." Good news to us was devastating news to Mom and scores of my Witness relatives, not only had we moved far away physically, we had abandoned "the only true religion."

According to Dad, Mom expressed her dismay about my spiritual decision to her therapist,

"How old is Dwight?" the therapist queried.

"Thirty-three," mom replied.

"He's over 21. He can decide for himself which religion he wants."

But it is not that simple for relatives of those leaving "the truth." Mom's dream of having her entire family together on a paradise earth was shattered. God would punish me for rebellion against God's organization, the Watchtower Society. Gloomily, Mom envisioned living on the paradise earth without me and my family. We would be annihilated forever.

Sadly, in the short term, Mom would not be allowed to invite me and Roselie into her home for family gatherings. Mom appeared heart-broken. Could she reverse my decision? Would she continue to try and bring me back into her sphere of influence and perhaps win me back to Watchtower beliefs, recanting my belief in Christ as my Lord and my God?

"Dwight, you know that new yellow house just down the road from our place? I can get that house for you if you move back here." I understood Mom's motive in trying to move us back closer to her. I think she wished to reform my "apostate" thinking, or at least influence our children with Witness ideals. We were strapped financially, living in a rented house, barely making ends meet. However, I felt no temptation to move to the nice yellow house. I had been set free of sin and guilt, I was forgiven. Why would I choose to re-enter a religious system where true forgiveness cannot be known, only hoped for? After a few months, I learned, the yellow house burned.

Eventually the mother-son phone conversations ceased all together.

My parents' visits were awkward, sitting in our living room, Mom focusing her conversation on our children, obediently shunning Roselie and me. Dad was more open with us. He had not been baptized, so the Witnesses couldn't disfellowship him for talking with us. He, by himself, visited several times, determined to maintain family ties, yet perturbed that I had upset Mom by getting disfellowshipped.

Our children loved Grandpa's solo visits. During one of those visits, our youngest, Amy (age 6), sitting on his lap, told him the story of Jesus, asking him to follow her in a prayer for Jesus to save him. She ran excitedly to Roselie "Papa just prayed and asked Jesus into his heart!"

While staying with us, Dad read a Christian testimony book, a woman changed by Christ. With tears in his eyes, he commented "I now see how the Trinity could be true." I doubt Dad ever told Mom of his experiences at our home, they would have been too upsetting for her.

We traveled to western New York visiting Roselie's family. Sometimes we would drive the extra ninety miles in hopes of seeing my family, occasionally visiting my dad's mom, Grandma Hayes, a Christian. One trip we had no place to spend the night. A cousin allowed us to visit in his home. Would he invite us to stay over? His dad (my uncle, a Witness elder) was aware of our presence. His dad phoned him during our two-hour visit, possibly reminding my cousin of the dangers of fraternizing with disfellowshipped family. After the call, I sensed a change in his attitude. Soon after, we set off into a cold winter night, for the twelve-hour-trip back to Virginia.

Somewhere in Pennsylvania, at a McDonalds, our seven-year old, Billy, spontaneously said, "I want to ask Jesus into my heart." He bowed his head at the yellow plastic-topped table, asking Jesus to come into his heart and save him. We were elated. Our Lord had shown himself to be the Light, even in the darkness of rejection.

After 1983 our business prospered. We purchased a motor home for trips north. I parked in my parent's driveway, all four children visited my Mom and Dad. Roselie and I remained in the R.V.

The children grew in age and maturity. The eldest, Karrie and Doug, now teenagers, answered Grandma's proselytizing attempts with Bible verses. Both youths were troubled, asking me, "How could Grandma say she is in the true religion and refuse to speak with her own son?"

Accidents plagued Dad. Once, his pelvis was crushed when he was trapped by rolling bundles of lumber. He was unloading a boxcar at the lumber company where he worked. We wore face masks and robes when visiting him in I.C.U. We entered a tiny room and prayed for him. Thankfully he recovered, returning to work.

I had volunteered to minister to the inmates in the local Jail. One Tuesday night, a guard entered the area and said,

"Your parents have just been in a serious traffic accident." As I prepared to leave the cell block, seven or eight sympathetic inmates promised to pray for my mom and dad.

I returned my sister Vonda's call.[12] She described the accident, Mom and Dad were in the hospital.

Rescue personnel, thinking Dad was dead, airlifted the other victims and rescued him last. Mom was in pain with bruised ribs, but would be released

---

[12] *Witnesses were permitted to talk to disfellowshipped family in crisis situations, but socializing or religious talk was forbidden.*

soon. Dad was in critical condition, if he survived he would be in the hospital a long time.

Thankfully the man and boy from the other crashed vehicle survived.

The tragedy literally opened the door to my parent's home. Mom was in her bed, in good spirits, looking great, but occasionally writhing in pain from injured ribs. Roselie and I were received graciously. I told Mom, "Jail inmates in Virginia are praying for you." Surprisingly she laughed and said she was glad. I thought, "Thank you Jesus! Even though Mom is on strong pain killers, perhaps not fully aware of her words, she for the moment appreciated prayers from non-Witnesses." I felt as if the inmate's prayers were a gift from God.

She completely recovered.

At the hospital, Dad looked bad but was still conscious. Roselie, Karrie, Doug, Billy, Amy and I circled his bed. As Billy played guitar, we sang "Amazing Grace" and prayed for Dad. I asked him if he was prepared to enter eternity, his pained answer, "I know you must believe." Surprisingly he once again recovered, although he remained handicapped and walked with assistance the rest of his life.

* * * *

My brother David's health had been declining for years. Finally, diabetes caused kidney failure, resulting in blindness. During a visit to Roselie's family in Western New York, my sister called informing me of his condition. He was hospitalized in Geneva, New York, about 100 miles away.

Lying in the hospital bed, he detailed his prognosis. His kidneys were barely functioning. His sight was slowly returning. He would need twice weekly dialysis. Another time, while ill, he had refused my offer to pray for him. So, I decided not to offer again. I called to mind Jesus' promise to those who believe, found in the Gospel of Mark, "... they will place their hands on sick people, and they will get well." (Mark 16:17,18).

I thought, "I'll silently pray for him anyway. He doesn't have to know what I'm doing. I don't have to make a grand speech to God." While he talked with his daughter, I moved closer. Placing my hands on his ankles, I prayed, secretly.

Trying to exit his hospital room on a humorous note, I joked, "When you get ready for a new kidney, let me know, I'll drop one off for you anytime." He quipped, "If I ever need one, I'll wait for a cadaver."

Three months later, he phoned, "Were you really serious when you offered me a kidney?"

"Of course," I replied without pause, inwardly wondering if I was actually making such a commitment.

"This dialysis is really rough, I have good insurance, it will cover a transplant. Are you sure? You'd better check with your family," he continued.

Without asking, I knew Roselie and our children's response, "Yes of course we should do this!"

I also sensed my Lord's hand in David's request. I was confident all the medical tests would be fine and the transplanted kidney fully compatible. A barrage of tests followed.

Within four months we signed-in at the University of Rochester's Transplant Center. Two evenings before the surgeries, walking to the hospital, I saw glimmering in the fading sunlight a little silver rhinestone cross. It was lying on the sidewalk. As I retrieved it I looked upward and saw a white fabric cross taped in a sixth or seventh floor window. I sensed God's smile on our mission.

As I was prepped for surgery the doctor asked why my older brother had requested no blood transfusions in the event of an emergency and why I made no such request. I explained that I too had once followed that thinking, having been one of Jehovah's Witnesses. Now with a differing view, I no longer believed blood transfusions to be an act of disobedience to God. Still I wasn't eager to receive a blood transfusion. He assured me that transfusions were rarely needed during this type surgery.

The Watchtower Society had condemned blood transfusions since 1945. Beginning in 1968, organ transplants had also been forbidden. The Society asserted that a patient's body somehow partially consumed the donor's organ, making the organ recipient guilty of cannibalism, making it an act of disobedience to God.

Thankfully, for my brother, the ban lasted only twelve years. The Watchtower Society had revoked that ruling seventeen years prior. Witnesses were now allowed to make their own choices regarding organ transplants.

Through a curtain, I heard David's elders wishing him their best. Shortly, a lady with a Russian accent began infusing white I.V. fluid into my arm. "Count to ten she said."

I consented, "One, two, three…"

Seemingly moments later a woman's voice said,

"Mr. Hayes, wake up, both you and your brother did well in surgery."

Five days in the hospital bed were not as fun as I thought they might be. I can now see why God put Adam into a deep sleep as He surgically removed his rib, creating Eve. Doctors sawed off part of my rib to make exit space for the kidney's removal.

Amid post-surgical pain and hallucinations from pain killers, a young Catholic priest appeared with a Gideon Bible in hand. I told him how, as a Jehovah's Witness, I had particularly despised Catholic doctrines. I realized now that Protestant and Catholic Christians believed in the same Christ. The young man easily found a Bible verse I'd been trying to locate for a long time, he read it, bringing me great comfort. "If you are insulted for the name of Christ, you are blessed, for the Spirit of glory and of God rests upon you." (1 Peter 4:14)

Just as the doctors had predicted; my brother began to look and feel better immediately. As my Lord would have it, ours was a 98% match. Only limited rejection medications would be required.

My relationship with David warmed considerably. After he recovered, he drove to Virginia. We celebrated his good health with his favorite, a (sugar free) root beer ice cream float.

Despite being a Witness elder, he did not continue to shun me. At times, he expressed his wish that I would come back to the Witnesses. But he listened with interest as I shared my faith in Jesus. I explained that Jesus has a gift waiting for all who believe, "for all have sinned and fallen short of the glory of God...for the wages of sin is death, but the gift of God is eternal life in Jesus Christ our Lord" (see Romans 3:23; 6:23).

David lived nearly nine additional years. Ultimately diabetes destroyed his heart, but his replacement kidney kept working until the end.

My son-in-law Wes and I traveled to see David on his deathbed. The kindly Hospice lady said, "David can hear everything you say, but he's unable to respond." A private opportunity presented itself just before his family gathered around him for the last time. Wes whispered the Biblical words: "Believe in the Lord Jesus and you will be saved" (see Acts 16:31). Wes urged David to trust Jesus with all his heart, asking Jesus for forgiveness of sins. Then in a quiet moment I wished him goodbye, pleading, "Trust Jesus, David, trust Jesus."

Wes and I began the long trip home to Virginia. I reflected on how formerly as a Witness, I had not believed a deathbed conversion was even possible. There would be no time left to take the necessary steps to inherit life.

Jehovah's Witnesses' thoughts about salvation went like this: dedicating one's life to God the Father, baptism by immersion, attending all meetings, witnessing house-to-house, living morally, obeying a multitude of Watchtower rules and praying for the Witness work worldwide.[13] God would then decide if I

---

[13] *The Watchtower path to everlasting life sometimes alluded to faith in the Jesus of the Watchtower as one of several vital steps, other times faith in their Christ was not mentioned at all. In either*

had done enough good works to survive his final war, the battle of Armageddon. Like school, you might narrowly receive a passing grade (life everlasting) and the student sitting next to you had one point less so he barely failed (annihilation). But thankfully as the Bible teaches,

"It is by grace you have been saved, through faith – and this not from yourselves, it is the gift of God..." (see Ephesians 2:8)

Just as the thief crucified next to Jesus believed during his dying moments, my brother David may have trusted that same Jesus on his deathbed. (see Luke 23:40-43)

These are my last memories of my Witness family.

* * * *

Back in Petra, Jordan, I shared my story with my newly discovered Irish and English brothers and sisters. They video-taped and I spoke of Jesus from my viewpoint both as a Jehovah's Witness and as a born-again believer. I told of my prayer to find the real Truth and how that prayer had been marvelously answered on August 3, 1980. I had experienced great emotion at my salvation encounter, but I explained that such a feeling is not required to believe. It is an extra blessing. Some of us are just hard-headed Irish and God gives us an extra confirmation, getting it into our thick skulls

---

case I can never recall the concept being explained in any meaningful way.

that we are saved. I now know that the Jesus of the Bible will completely save all those who believe.

Soon a guide signaled, "Time to leave." The cameras were clicked off, the men shook my hand, the women kissed my cheek. The last person, a young woman said, "For a long time I've been confused about whether Christ could completely save me. Also, I've never had an emotional salvation experience as many of my friends have. This very morning, I prayed that today God would settle all my doubts. He sent you here in answer to my prayer. I am now confident in my Christian faith."

I stood there thinking, "I'm here beholding one of the wonders of the ancient world, yet Lord, your Spirit working in people's hearts is far more wonderful than this remarkable place. Thank you Lord for my family in Christ."

I wished I had gotten their names. Would I ever see these people again?

Yes, and I would not have to wait long. By providence, we would again meet the very next day, at the Dead Sea in Israel.

Chapter 14
Baptism and Discipleship

"Therefore go and make disciples of all nations, baptizing them in the name of the Father and of the Son and of the Holy Spirit," Matthew 28:19

White-robed baptismal candidates were being immersed. Others were being were sprinkled or poured on. A variety of Christian denominations were represented. Leaders read scripture and prayed. Blessings were pronounced and songs sung. The scenario is repeated daily. Devout pilgrims seek baptism in the Jordan, the same river where Jesus was baptized. On my Holy Land trips, I never cease to be impressed by the number and sincerity of those gathered by the river awaiting baptism.

I was reminded of the spring day in 1981 when my wife, myself and our two eldest children waded into a rural stream. Like Israel's famous river, the creek was named "The Jordan River."

At last Roselie and I were free with no more guilt feelings or fear of death. We were no longer subject to authoritarian religious leadership and a plethora of man-made rules. We were no longer working to please God in exchange for everlasting life. We had accepted God's forgiveness. We knew we were pardoned of our sins. We knew from his promise that we have eternal life. "For God so loved the world that he gave his one and only Son, that *whoever believes* in him shall not perish but have eternal life" (see John 3:16 Italics added). We, by God's grace, were new believers in

Christ but we wanted to be baptized and become his disciples, following in Jesus' footsteps.

For years, I had a reoccurring dream. I was in a car group of Witnesses. The next house was my turn. As I approached the door I would think, "I can't introduce myself as a Jehovah's Witness! What will I tell the householder? Should I explain the true gospel? What will the car captain do if he finds me out; telling people they need to be born again?" I would awake each time from the nightmarish scenario just as I rang the doorbell.

Grasping the magnitude of my freedom took time. I had become used to submitting to a strong controlling organization. I caught myself wondering "Who will tell us what to do now?" I knew I must find other freedom loving Christians with which to fellowship, people who cherished their liberty in Christ as I did.

Our first church experience was with the folks at the nondenominational Western Light Tabernacle in Moneta, Virginia. The people were committed to Christ and sincere in devotion, loving, and accepting of our family. They sang the old gospel hymns all of which I was hearing for the first time. If there was a need, members gathered around to help. They cherished meal times together, "dinner on the grounds" as it was called. We spent a blessed year with them.

On a warm June afternoon following the Sunday morning Tabernacle service, the congregation, Pastor Clayton Leonard, our Atlanta friends Judy and Gary, and our family proceeded to Holy Land USA. The 190-acre representation of ancient Israel was located in Bedford, County, Virginia, only a few miles from the Tabernacle. With young and old alike, we walked the half-mile gravel lane to the "Jordan River," a bold country stream flowing over a scenic waterfall and then swirling into a deep pool.

Karrie (age 12), Doug (age 9), Roselie and I followed Preacher Clayton, into a rain swollen pool of muddy reddish-brown, waist-deep water. After preaching and praying he immersed each of us, lowering us backwards into the water, "I baptize you in the name of the Father, and of the Son, and of the Holy Ghost. Buried in the likeness of his death; raised in the likeness of his resurrection," The Preacher declared.

The crowd sang the old hymn, "Shall We Gather by The River."

As Witnesses, baptism was thought to be an essential step. One could not expect to enter everlasting life without it. Now I understood baptism to be a sign that one had decided to follow Jesus (see Mark 16:16). We authentically bore the name "Christian." Baptism publicly identified us with Jesus.

During the preceding months, both Karrie and Doug had also placed their faith in Jesus. They chose to be baptized with Roselie and me. Since none of our children had been baptized as Jehovah's Witnesses, they could not be disfellowshipped for turning away from "the truth." Witness acquaintances could continue to speak with them if they chose. Nonetheless most Witnesses shunned them too. Karrie shared later, "It was like death, the loss of grandparents, aunts, uncles and cousins – lots and lots of grief."

Judy and Gary stayed a few days after our baptism, encouraging and praying for us. Gary commented on the sparkle in our three-year-old Amy's eyes. "I believe she'll be an evangelist someday," He said. Our landlord Mr. Brown was likewise captivated by those same eyes, one green, one blue. "I think she'll be a doctor one day," he told me. "I can see it in her eyes." Both predictions would prove true.

We would see Judy one more time. Four years earlier, I, as inquisitor, had questioned Judy's newfound faith in Jesus and ordered her disfellowshipping. This woman's peaceful spirit had touched Roselie and me again and again. She and Gary were now blessing the one who had banished them.

Following our baptism in the "Jordan River," we continued several more months in fellowship at the Tabernacle. But I had so many theological questions. I am deeply grateful for the folks at Western Light Tabernacle. Their hospitality, singing and preaching were an unspeakable blessing. But I hungered for more details, the how, whys and wherefores. I longed for a mentor to take me into the breadth of Christian theology.

We met Dr. Jerry Stiles, founder of a summer youth ministry, Aletheia Springs Christian Education Center, in Ferrum, Virginia. The small but devoted church held meetings on campus.

Though nondenominational in structure, the fellowship followed the Plymouth Brethren worship model. Anglo-Irish evangelist John N. Darby (1800 - 1882) of Plymouth, England, proclaimed the Bible's emphasis on the literal fulfillment of Bible prophecies, an actual return of Jews to their Palestinian homeland and a special place in God's heart for the Jewish people. Darby also taught an imminent "rapture" of the church, the belief that followers of Jesus will be suddenly taken to heaven at any moment, followed by a seven-year time of tribulation and then Christ's return and his literal millennial (1000 year) reign on earth.

Other believers not connected to Darby, and unknown to each other, arrived at similar conclusions. This spontaneous movement made an indelible mark on Protestant Christianity. Evangelicals particularly took notice of Darby's observations when re-gathered Israel declared its statehood, May 16, 1948.

Dr. Stiles answers were Biblically-based. He showed me more than a hundred Bible verses clearly identifying Jesus with Jehovah of the Old Testament. For example, Jehovah is called the Rock in one verse and Jesus is called the Rock in another.

"There is no one holy like Jehovah, for there is no one but you; And there is no rock like our God" (1 Samuel 2:2NWT).

"... for they [Israelites] drank of that spiritual Rock that followed them: and that Rock was Christ" (1 Corinthians 10:4 KJV).

One more example, Jehovah is called King in one verse and Jesus is called King in another.

"But Jehovah is in truth God. He is the living God and the King to time indefinite...." (Jeremiah 10:10 NWT)

"And he [Jesus] hath on his vesture and on his thigh a name written, KING OF KINGS, AND LORD OF LORDS." (Revelation 19:16 KJV)

As a Jehovah's Witness, I had been taught that the Holy Spirit is God's invisible active force like electricity, impersonal. Jerry explained the Christian view. He showed me 32 verses demonstrating the personality of the Holy Spirit, a living divine Person, the same essence as God. An example, "... no one knows the thoughts of God except the Spirit of God." (1 Corinthians 2:11b)

The Holy Spirit possesses knowledge. An impersonal force could not know the "thoughts of God," Jerry explained.

And the Holy Spirit is called "God" in the Bible, "Then Peter said... you have lied to the Holy Spirit... You have not lied to men but to God" (see Acts 5: 3,5).

Jerry taught on the doctrine of the Holy Trinity. He illustrated God's triune nature through a study of God's attributes. To list just a few, God the Father, God the Son, and God the Holy Spirit all share: God's omnipotence, (all-powerfulness) His omniscience, (all-knowingness - past, present, future) His omnipresence, (present everywhere at all times) and His eternalness. (always existing, without beginning or end)

Jerry presented extensive scriptural proofs of the Trinity using these four attributes. Here is an example: The Father is all knowing: "Your Father knows what you need before you ask him" (Matthew 6:8). "Are not two sparrows sold for a penny? Yet not one of them will fall to the ground apart from the will of your Father. And even the very hairs of your head are numbered" (Matthew 10:29-30).

Christ the Son is all knowing: "Now we can see that you [Jesus] know all things..." (John 16:30) And the Holy Spirit is all knowing: "The Spirit searches all things, even the deep things of God." (1 Corinthians 2:10b) "In the same way no one knows the thoughts of God except the Spirit of God" (1 Corinthians 2:11b).

Jerry explained, "Christians have one God. We are monotheistic. We believe three persons: Father, Son, and Holy Spirit, coexist in one essence, God. We call this the triune nature of God." We are made in the image of God. The Bible speaks of our body, soul, spirit

– yet we still are each a single human being" (see Genesis 1:27; Hebrews 4:12).

"At baptism, we always recite Jesus' statement which also proves the Trinity," Dr. Stiles continued. "We say, 'I baptize you in the name of the Father and of the Son and of the Holy Spirit,' not three separate names but a single name, the name of God; three persons in one with one name, God" (see Matthew 28:19).

As Jerry Stiles mentored Roselie and me, his wife Judy instilled in our children a vibrant love for Jesus. She used enthusiastic Bible teaching and singing.

My home-based business couldn't keep up with the growing financial needs of our family. I needed a job to support our family of six. The church at Aletheia Springs prayed for me, to get a job. That same week I received a call from Roanoke. Would I be interested in working for Ewald-Clark, a camera store? They were installing the city's first one-hour photo lab. Would I consider managing the new enterprise? I had purchased a few supplies from their store; but they really didn't know me well. The new job was definitely an answer to prayer.

Managing the camera section of the store was Buddy Dooley, a Christian. We became close friends, visiting in each other's homes. His wife Debbie and Roselie enjoyed discussing the children. We committed to pray for their daughter, Rosy, who when subjected to loud noises like sirens or low flying aircraft suffered anxiety attacks. The Dooley home was situated squarely beneath the airport's landing approach. Passenger planes continually roared over their house. Happily, God would answer that prayer as we shall later see.

Eventually I left Ewald-Clark, returning to self-employment. Buddy and Debbie moved to the desert Southwest. With the entire country between us, would we ever meet again?

By late 1983 the thirty-three-mile trip to worship at Aletheia Springs became too difficult. Our son Billy (age 5) would get car-sick from the winding roads. We couldn't make it for midweek services and local community outreach. We tried but couldn't find property in the Ferrum area.

We decided to visit a Rocky Mount church, at about half the distance we were traveling. At school, our daughter Karrie (age 15) had heard about the Franklin Heights Baptist Church's youth program. We visited the church. She and Doug (age 13) immediately liked Mark Griffith, the youth minister. We joined the church. Recently Karrie shared, "Mark and Kathy (Mark's wife) helped me become more normal. He helped me stand up and be different when I needed to. As a Witness, I was always different all the time, now when I needed to stand up and be different; it was out of obedience to Jesus."

I perceived the church's pastor, Larry Holland, to be a strong leader, still he did not drive the flock. I recalled as a child, when my dad asked me to go round-up our sheep, I'd get behind the flock and try to drive them to the barn. The more I tried, the more they scattered, and the madder I got. I discovered if I could get the lead-sheep to eat from my little bucket of oats and follow me, the entire flock would follow her and we would all get to the barn. Pastor Holland seemed to shepherd the flock like that. He patiently developed leaders. He let church staff, deacons, and teachers lead and still he was quick to deal with problems that might disunite the flock. His sermon series which most impacted me was, "Dying to Self and Living with Resurrection Power."

In an era stained by the moral failures of prominent Christian leaders, both Pastor Holland and Mark Griffith set an excellent example in their personal lives.

When we started attending Franklin Heights in 1983, Sunday morning attendance averaged about three hundred. Today the average is over eleven hundred. I believe the church's growth can be attributed to lifting-up the name of Jesus in music, preaching, and teaching.

As our youngest, Billy and Amy, made professions of faith in Christ they were baptized in the crystal-clear water of Franklin Heights' indoor baptismal pool. They were discipled by Mark Griffith.

* * * *

Back at Israel's Jordan River, it was time to move on. I climbed steps leading to the bath house, hearing harmonious singing fade into the background. It was time to shower, change back into dry clothes and board the bus, continuing our Holy Land tour.

Chapter 15
Reunited

"But Esau ran to meet Jacob and embraced him; he threw his arms around his neck and kissed him"
Genesis 33:4.

On a pleasant November day in 2010 we departed Petra, the ancient home of Esau. Traveling over 100 miles we descended 4,000 feet to sea level at the Red Sea, passing by Lawrence of Arabia's Valley of the Moon and through wilderness where the Israelites wandered. Our overnight destination was Eliat, Israel. Four countries converge at Eliat, Saudi Arabia, Egypt, Jordan, and Israel.

Reflecting on my meeting with Irish and English Christians at Petra's famous Treasury, (see Chapter 13) I wished I'd had more time to talk and gotten names. I longed to see them again.

Twenty-five years earlier I had longed to see Christian friends another time. God granted the desire of my heart.

One day, Roselie held a parchment card. "It's an invitation to a wedding in Atlanta. Can we go? The celebration is at the Hyatt Grande Hotel." We had met the bride in Western New York. She had moved to Atlanta and was getting married. Like us, she was an ex-Witness and a born-again Christian.

"Yes, let's go. It's about four hundred miles." I said. "We can take the RV and camp. We'll make reservations at Stone Mountain Park campsite. We can see Judy and Gary again."

We arrived in Atlanta. Hours before the wedding we still had not shopped for a wedding gift. "Look, here's a plaza, and I think see a gift shop!" Roselie said excitedly. I pulled our motor home into the plaza. We got out. As we walked towards the gift shop, a woman in the parking lot looked me straight in the eyes and exclaimed "Dwight Hayes!" I took a second look "Debbie Dooley! What are you doing here? You live in the desert!"

"We moved here from Arizona, what are you and your family doing here?"

"We're headed into that gift shop to buy a wedding present. We're on our way to a wedding in downtown Atlanta."

"I own that gift shop and another one too. That's where Buddy is right now. Come in; I'll help you find a gift and wrap it too."

We found a lovely gift, but Debbie kept urging Billy and Amy to put this toy and that game into the shopping cart. Roselie and I were thinking the same thing, "How are we going to pay for all this?" As we rolled up to the check-out, Debbie said "Roselie, close your purse. Remember that time in Roanoke when we were so broke? You helped us out just in time. Everything in this store is yours."

We arranged to meet Buddy and Debbie at Stone Mountain Lake, the next morning.

The wedding and reception were beautiful. Many of the attendees were former Jehovah's Witnesses, disfellowshipped for their faith in Christ. I sensed a wonderful camaraderie among the guests.

There we saw Helen Ortega who had earnestly prayed for Roselie's conversion. Helen had nurtured Roselie during the early weeks of her search for the truth.

I was introduced to Raymond Franz (1922-2010) former Governing Body member at the Watchtower's world headquarters in Brooklyn, NY. He left the Witnesses in 1980, the same year as me. He was disfellowshipped for questioning the Governing Body's authoritarian leadership. His scholarly books *Crisis of Conscience* (1983) and *In Search of Christian Freedom* (1991) give an insider's view of his long-time association within the nucleus of the Watchtower Society.

Once again, we conversed with David Henke, founder of Watchman Fellowship, a ministry which offers information on religious cults. Today that organization is a nationally recognized authority on such groups.

We dined in style with Judy and Gary, surrounded by a myriad of new friends. With joyful music and laughter all about us, the bride and groom waltzed into a star-filled Atlanta night.

The next morning at Stone Mountain Lake we relaxed in the warm sunshine, with Buddy and Debbie at our side. We recalled memories from the Roanoke camera store and updated each other on our families. The kids pedaled paddle boats and tossed bread to the swans.

"Buddy, does Rosy still panic when she hears loud sounds, like she used to?" I asked.

"Why no, she hasn't done that since we lived in Roanoke." He answered. Secret joy flooded my heart,

Roselie and I had been burdened for their little girl, praying for Jesus to take away her anxiety.

"That's good news," I replied. I recalled as a Jehovah's Witness I did not pray for an individual's healing. Most prayers were nonspecific, asking God to protect the worldwide Watchtower organization.

It was a heavenly moment, I pinched myself (yes actually pinched myself) to see if we were still in the mortal realm. "I wonder if we were killed on I-85 on our way here and we're already in heaven right now?" I asked out loud. Roselie reminded me she'd had a severe food allergy reaction the prior night; we were not in heaven yet!

Though we did not realize it then, the evening before we had seen beloved Judy for the last time. A few months later Gary phoned, he described Judy's peaceful farewell. She was overflowing with love and joy up to her last breath, leaving behind him and their two children. Her forty-year-old body was devastated by breast cancer.

Next time we see Judy, it will be at a site lovelier than Stone Mountain Lake, a finer place than Hyatt's Grande Hotel. I can only imagine that glorious meeting with Jesus and the joy of seeing Judy again.

* * * *

After a good night's rest in Eliat, Israel, our tour bus made the long trip through the Negev desert to the Dead Sea. We pulled into one of the Dead Sea's several beaches.

Recovering from a cold I decided not to get wet this time. I stood on shore taking pictures of others floating in the briny water. From a distance, someone called, "Sir, you're the man we talked with yesterday in Petra." I looked up to see one of the Irish couples I had chatted with just the day before.

"Would you mind coming up to our bus and speak with our people?" they asked. "Your testimony we taped yesterday is already being sent around the UK on the internet."

We have experienced numerous rejections from former Witness family and acquaintances. But our Lord has always responded by providing loving brothers and sisters. In contrast to the loving Christians I met in Petra and saw again in Israel. I have been ignored by Witnesses at business meetings, a Witness couple vacated their reserved seats at a dinner theater to escape sitting face-to-face with Roselie's and me, and I have been angrily chased from the parking lot surrounding a Witness convention for trying to share the gospel. Though Witnesses are informed of my address, they have mistakenly called at our home, only to silently turn and leave when we opened our door. Attending relatives' funerals at the Kingdom Hall would have been intimidating were it not for God lovingly sending a handful of Christian relatives to comfort us in a crowd of Witnesses. For every rejection we have faced, Jesus has blessed us with a multitude of loving relationships.

Chapter 16
"Dwight, Trust Me!"

"...they should always pray and not give up." Luke 18:1

Day three (see Chapters 5 and 7) on the 40-mile Jesus Trail, found Jerry and me descending from the Horns of Hattin into a valley called Nakhal Arbel. Now well below sea level we continued following orange trail blazes through countless olive groves. The sky was bright and the sun warm. I had drunk plenty of water. But that afternoon, miles away from civilization I noticed what appeared to be blood in my urine. I nervously tried to forget what I'd seen, but later the urine was even redder. I prayed silently: "Lord, I'm worried about blood in my urine."

These words came to mind, "Dwight stop worrying. You can trust Me. I will never leave you or forsake you."

"OK, Lord I trust you, I won't worry." Minutes later I found myself worrying again. "But Lord I have only one kidney; what if it's a kidney problem?"

Once again, only now more firmly, the same words were impressed on my mind. "Dwight stop worrying! You can trust Me. I will never leave you or forsake you."

I struggled not to think about it again, even though the problem continued through that day and on through the next and last hiking day.

Most of my Jesus Trail meditations had been brief heavenward communiqués. Like: "Lord I am impressed with the beauty of these cliffs "or" thank you for keeping my foot from stumbling or Jesus you must have rested after you walked that arduous stretch." My physical need appeared urgent; yet I felt secure because of the One watching over me. More than two decades earlier our family had learned to pray out of necessity. Our needs were great, and our blessings were huge. Gathering in our living room we would pray for: our car to run, money to pay bills, and enough firewood to warm our house. We tired of being miserable complainers and somehow God gave us the grace to be more thankful for everything including, during lean times, lentil pea soup.

Though God does not always answer my prayers in the way I expect, here are some examples of his graciousness.

I have been meeting for weekly prayer with friends, Doyle and Danny. We have been meeting for over twenty years. I once needed $2,500 by week's end for business taxes. We prayed. A couple of days later a whole sale client came and paid his monthly bill. It totaled $1,400 but he wrote a check for $2,500. Roselie said "You only owe $1,400." He answered, "Yes I know, but I have the extra right now so I'm paying some in advance." He had never done that before nor did he ever again.

Jehovah's Witnesses warned their people if they left "the truth," their children would become worldly and fall victim to the evils promoted by the culture. Especially harmful was a college education. In particular, the study of philosophy would destroy a person's spirituality, it was claimed. While college was discouraged, military service was forbidden. Any Witness serving would be disassociated, punishment almost identical to disfellowshipping.

At Dad's funeral, former Witness friends appeared mystified to see our four grown children looking clean cut and respectable. Our kids, the children of evil "apostates," contradicted the long-held notion that those defecting from Jehovah's Witnesses were doomed to a life of debauchery.

Quite the contrary has occurred.

Throughout her teen years, our eldest daughter Karrie, endured considerable rejection from Witness classmates and family. Only recently has she shared some of those feelings. I am convinced that her rejection experiences have contributed to her maturity as an adult. She views all family relationships as vital. She desires her children to be closely knit with grandparents, aunts, uncles, and cousins.

Karrie has empathy for youth. She told me of a mom and her twelve-year old son. They were visiting her home as Jehovah's Witnesses. Karrie said, "I commented to the lady, 'I really feel sorry for your son. I understand how hard it is to be a Jehovah's Witness kid in the school system. Being twelve years old is hard because you are awkward and goofy anyway but when you throw in extreme religious differences it makes it even harder.' I asked her if she'd been a Jehovah's Witness as a child. She told me she'd grown up in a Baptist church and then converted to the Witnesses as an adult. I told her that she'd had a choice and her son did not.

"Her twelve-year-old appeared absolutely miserable. I tried to engage him in conversation, but his mother typically would answer for him. The young man was a middle school student. I asked him if he liked school and he replied, 'No! I hate it. I would rather die than go back.' His mom brushed off his comments and they left soon after."

My daughter's story reminded me of my own distaste for school. I cannot recall even one day in all my school years when I wanted to go to school. It was not pleasant being bullied and punched by kids whose parents despised Jehovah's Witnesses.

Karrie works as a Nuclear Medicine Technologist. She and her husband have three children. They serve in their local church.

At age ten, our son Doug performed a solo at the Tabernacle. Strumming his guitar, he sang, "What a Friend We Have in Jesus." He continually encouraged neighborhood kids to come to Bible Study and church.

While working on the railroad, he took college classes. Later I joined him for a few seminary classes, like Christology, Anthropology, and Youth Ministry. After ten years on the railroad he applied for position of Youth Minister at our church. Mark Griffith was moving into another role, Minister of Education.

For nearly a dozen years he has been Youth Minister. As I reflect, I was never a teenager. I do not know what it is like to be one. I was perpetually an adult, toting my witnessing case filled with Watchtower literature, ready to prove to anyone that the teachings of the church were of the devil and that only Jehovah's Witnesses had the truth. Doug, however, had been a teenager. He understood teens. Mark Griffith had mentored him throughout his teen years.

I think of our younger son Billy as a prayer warrior. He believed, without doubting, that God would answer his prayers. Whether asking God to hold back a rainstorm until we arrived at our destination with a broken car window or praying and fasting that God would stop the occult activities of a fellow elementary school classmate. God seemed to hear and answer the child's prayers with remarkable certainty.

We and other parents assembled for a children's program at church. Billy got up to recite his short verse. His words escaped him. Standing there for a long moment, he returned to his seat. I thought, "Oh no, this will embarrass him, he will never again be able to speak in front of a crowd. Lord please help Billy not to be afraid."

Ten years later Bill served in the Army's 82nd Airborne jazz band. He performed for Ross Perot and Madeline Albright. Once he played guitar and sang alongside singer Wayne Newton.

Bill is employed at a veteran's hospital, counseling patients with mental illness issues. He married Wendy, a lovely southern belle and gifted singer. They have three children. They share their musical talents in their church.

Our Atlanta friend, Gary said he thought Amy would be an evangelist someday and our landlord had seen in her eyes the making of a doctor. Both predictions about our younger daughter were to come true.

She evangelized on church mission trips led by Youth Pastor Mark Griffith. Sometimes they went to inner city ghettos, other times to native Americans in rural settings. During college, she spent summer weeks on medical mission to help displaced people dwelling in Mexico's garbage dumps. During her last college break she worked on a medical team in Nepal. While in medical school she traveled to Malawi in Africa and again Mexico City. During residency, she endured the jungles of Papua New Guinea and flew to Indonesia for tsunami relief. She visited other countries where Christianity is forbidden, at times meeting secretly with underground believers.

I remember a phone call, "Dad, I can't even mention His [Jesus] name here," she whispered. "There are armed guards watching me as I examine patients, all I can do is lay my hands on the patients as He [Jesus] would." Amy routinely asks her patients if she may pray for them. I knew she was silently praying for her patients' healing, even Islam's Sharia law could not bar prayers from reaching the Christian God.

Amy, now a family practice physician, and her gynecologist husband, Derek, hope to open a women's clinic in an eastern African country. They have personally witnessed the pitiable state of women's health there. It's a country where the gospel of Jesus will change lives despite official opposition to evangelical Christianity.

* * * *

Returning to Israel's Jesus Trail: Exhausted and weak, yet triumphant, Jerry and I grabbed hold of the iron gate. Its sign read CAPHARNAUM THE TOWN OF JESUS. We had arrived at our forty-mile destination in four days, Nazareth to Capernaum. We had hiked the Jesus Trail arriving one hour earlier than expected. I collapsed on a stone bench while Jerry explored the ancient home of Jesus and Peter. Jesus had adopted Capernaum after being banished from his native Nazareth. My head swirled with exciting trail memories, as my body fell asleep.

Back in the U.S. my doctor said, "Myoglobin is secreted from overworked muscles, it looks like blood in the urine, actually it is harmless." As always, my Lord had proved trustworthy.

Part 2

Chapter 17
Did the Church Need Restoration?

"... upon this rock I will build my church, and the gates of hell shall not prevail against it" (Matthew 16:18 KJV)

I climbed back into the tour bus, my mind in deep reflection. The vehicle blurred past giant fig trees, as we departed Caesarea Philippi, the site where these words were spoken, "'But whom say ye that I [Jesus] am?' And Simon Peter answered and said, "Thou art the Christ, the Son of the living God." And Jesus answered and said unto him, "Blessed art thou, Simon Barjona: for flesh and blood hath not revealed it unto thee, but my Father which is heaven. And I say unto thee, that thou art Peter, and upon this rock I will build my church, and the gates of hell shall not prevail against it" (Matthew 16:15-18 KJV).

Tour host Micah had read those verses. And then closing his Bible, he said, "As our Lord Jesus spoke those words he possibly pointed towards that huge chasm in the cliff, 'the gates of hell,' as the Greeks called it. Jesus promised nothing would ever defeat his church; she would remain intact until he calls her home to heaven."

Micah was pointing to where, in Jesus' day, the Greeks had a temple honoring their god Pan, the half-man half-goat god of nature, a god which supposedly frightened and terrorized enemies (hence the word panic). They believed Pan was born in that chasm, the entrance to hell. Today only ruins of a temple remain, exposing the mouth of the bottomless pit.[14] As a Witness, I believed that Jesus had permitted his church to sink so low into corruption, so far from truth and rife with false doctrines that she needed a total restoration. And God chose Watchtower founder C.T. Russell, in 1884, to implement that restoration. How could I have accepted that proposition when Jesus said even the "gates of hell" would not overcome his church? I had chosen to accept the Watchtower's position as church-restorer rather than Jesus statement that his church would never sink so low as to need restoration.

Russell was not unique in attempting to restore the true church. Other newly formed unorthodox religious groups of the 19th century made similar claims. They also alleged that the church had failed, and that they alone were chosen of God to bring about its modern-day restoration.

I am convinced that church history, which was not taught to Jehovah's Witnesses in any meaningful way, validates Jesus' words. The church never was defeated but triumphed in the world through all generations. It was never overcome by the gates of hell. I believe God used reformers (not restorers) to spearhead the church's reformation (not restoration). The consecrated reformers never considered rejecting the precious doctrines that "restorationists" like Russell discarded as an abomination: historic doctrines such as the deity of Jesus Christ, his bodily resurrection, the immortality of the human soul, and the personality of the Holy Spirit.

---

[14] *Immeasurably deep according to Jewish historian Josephus.*

Reformer Luther wrote: "God wonderfully preserved his Gospel in the Church, which now [16th century] from the pulpits is taught to the people, word by word. In like manner, it is a special great work of God, that the creed, the Lord's Prayer, Baptism, and the Lord's Supper, have remained and cleaved to the hearts of those who were ordained to receive them amid Popedom."[15]

Luther claimed that God "preserved his Gospel in the Church" despite Roman Catholic excesses and heresies which he labeled "Popedom."

Why would the gates of hell attempt to overcome the church? The Bible reveals a scenario in an unseen realm. "Put on the full armor of God so you can take your stand against the devil's schemes. For our struggle is not against flesh and blood, but against the powers of this dark world and against the spiritual forces of evil in the heavenly realms. Therefore, put on the full armor of God, so that when the day of evil comes you may be able to stand your ground..." (Ephesians 6:11-13 italics added). Is there a conspiracy contrived by evil spirits to discredit Jesus as God and destroy his church, replacing God's grace at the cross with idolatrous "filthy rags" of salvation-by-human effort? (see Isaiah 64:6) Do Jehovah's Witnesses play a role in such an evil conspiracy? Jehovah's Witnesses are a miniscule group, merely seven million adherents, growing more slowly than the world's population. Yet I believe because they oppose Christ's church, they play a significant role in the devil's scheme.

---

[15] *From Luther's Table Talk quoted by Dr. Norman Geisler, Systematic Theology (Vol. 4, pg. 61).*

Jehovah's Witnesses distribute nearly 160 million copies of the *Watchtower and Awake!* magazine every month. These two periodicals and millions of other Watchtower books, booklets and tracts are distributed with a persistent theme, the church has failed, it is condemned, it is a tool of the devil and only Jehovah's Witnesses bear a restored message of truth.

For every individual professing to be a Jehovah's Witness there are dozens of non-Witnesses who have been influenced by Watchtower antichurch teachings; these people accept Watchtower beliefs which make them feel good but reject Witness doctrines which they find repulsive. For example, they feel good about rejecting Jesus' teaching on judgment and hell (see Matthew 25:46). They imagine no deceased relatives being punished in a literal hell as they have heard from Jehovah's Witnesses and their literature. But that same person who is sympathetic to many Watchtower doctrines is not ready to accept Witness teaching on blood transfusions. They would not let their child die for lack of a blood transfusion (refusal of blood transfusions being unique to Jehovah's Witnesses).

I call this the "residual effect." Palatable ideas linger on long after one has stopped involvement with Jehovah's Witnesses while unpalatable Watchtower doctrines are rejected. The net effect is that 7 million people spread the Watchtower's antichurch gospel, thinking of themselves as the only ones awaiting everlasting reward for their good works, but tens of millions identify themselves with some Witness teachings, doctrines they find likeable and logical. Paul warned that the days would come when "... they will want someone to tickle their own fancies, and they will collect teachers who pander to their own desires. They will no longer listen to the truth, but will wander off after man-made fictions" (see 2 Timothy 4:3,4; J.B. Phillips Translation).

This is a personal example of the residual effect. Several times my wife and I have counseled people in the following situation: a man marries a woman who grew up somehow connected to Jehovah's Witnesses; perhaps a grandmother witnessed to her as a child. She never committed to becoming a Jehovah's Witness. Now years into marriage the woman has developed an interest in spiritual matters, slowly she returns to the religious memories of her childhood. The first alarm goes off when the husband discovers that his wife has begun to "study" with the Witnesses. She begins to question the rightness of celebrating birthdays or Christmas. He envisions an unpleasant life without these special events and calls on us. He wants us to discourage his wife from further involvement with Jehovah's Witnesses. We meet with the couple. I urge the husband to launch his own search for God and truth, assuming spiritual leadership in his home (see 1 Corinthians 11:3). Unfortunately, the husband often has no interest in spiritual things. Therefore, he may choose to endure the discomfort of having his wife pursue Watchtower beliefs. Oddly, I have even had the pro-Witness wife agree with me, begging her husband to become their home's spiritual leader, seeking God. Other times the husband follows his wife into the Jehovah's Witnesses. Still other times divorce follows. Occasionally our advice was heeded, those families are now united in Christ, the husband accepting his role as spiritual leader.

As a former adherent of the Watchtower, I once was part of this ungodly collusion. I unwittingly conspired against Jesus and his church. I mistreated those Witnesses proclaiming themselves to be born again, identifying themselves as members of Christ's body, choosing like Thomas the apostle, to accept Jesus as "My Lord and my God." Often their family's connections were damaged or destroyed. My actions were always in harmony with organizational instructions, which I obeyed without question. My deeds were reprehensible. I ignorantly tried to damage Christ's church, yet upon turning to Jesus, he lovingly accepted me as part of his body (see 1 Corinthians 12:27). His church will never be overcome by the gates of hell.

* * * *

Perhaps a few people still journey to Caesarea Philippi to honor the almost forgotten Greek god Pan. Just a few weathered rocks of his once glorious temple remain. Pan was highly esteemed. But the man who revealed himself as Messiah, perhaps just a stone's throw from Pan's edifice, is esteemed by two billion people. Jesus' followers by the thousands come to the holy site to worship Him, they know little of the Greek god of nature and fright, Pan.

Chapter 18
Judgment and Hell

"Felix trembled..." Acts 24:25 KJV

"Felix was afraid..." Acts 24:25 NIV

"Felix became frightened..." Acts 24:25 NASB

"Felix was alarmed..." Acts 24:25 RSV

"Felix was terrified..." Acts 24:25 LB

"It was right here at Caesarea Maritima that Paul was imprisoned. He was incarcerated for three years. The governor's palace was located to your left, further out on the peninsula, surrounded by the Great Sea (Mediterranean). Governor Felix interviewed Paul in the Palace. Today its ruins are a favorite spot for fly fishermen," explained our Israeli guide, Izzy, as he enthusiastically pointed out ancient Caesarea's points of interest. Our tour group had gathered around the Pontius Pilate Stone, an inscribed rock verifying the existence of the Roman governor in Jesus' time. Behind us lay the possible location of Cornelius' house, an Italian soldier in the Roman army, the first Gentile to become a Christian. Moments before we walked through dark tunnels entering a massive Roman theater, centered around its judgment seat or "bema." Paul's word picture for the coming judgment of Christians (see 2 Corinthians 5:10).

I scanned the ruins of Caesarea's ancient palace. Fishermen were casting their hooks into a blue sea, surf sprayed white foam over their heads. I reflected on Paul's trial here, and I wondered about his audience with Roman Governor Felix. I thought back 30 years when a simple Bible phrase had forever reversed my thinking on the afterlife.

In the summer of 1980 I was processing photographs in my darkroom, a new believer in Jesus hungrily devouring the Bible. The book of Acts was playing on my cassette recorder; suddenly these words struck me, "Felix trembled."

I rewound the tape and played it again. When I did, it was like a light coming on in my head. The Bible text played once again, "He [Felix] sent for Paul, and listened to him as he spoke about faith in Christ Jesus. As Paul discoursed on righteousness, self-control, and the judgment to come, *Felix was afraid* and said, 'That's enough for now! You may leave. When I find it convenient, I will send for you' (see Acts 24:24,25 Italics mine)."

The Bible translation I was playing that day read, "Felix trembled." Felix was a tough Roman official. What on earth could make him afraid to the point of trembling? Certainly not the fear of dying, Roman officials lived in a violent world, surely the governor had settled any anxiety over dying. What struck me was Felix's extreme fear of "the judgment to come."

For the first time in my life I thought, hell must be real! Felix was not afraid of dying. He would not have been afraid of an unconscious eternity. Rather he must have been afraid of the punishment of hell. Paul's description of the judgment to come certainly included a future place of conscious discomfort, and just when the Governor began to feel the heat he dismissed Paul until a more convenient time.

As a Jehovah's Witness, I had been taught there was no conscious hell. We believed the righteous dead remained asleep until resurrection. We viewed with disdain all who taught the doctrine of hell "... the clergymen attribute to God, who is love, the wicked crime of torturing human creatures ..." (See Watchtower book "Let God be True," 1952 pg. 99).

We were instructed, "The doctrine of a burning hell where the wicked are tortured eternally after death cannot be true, mainly for four reasons: **(1) It is wholly unscriptural; (2) it is unreasonable; (3) it is contrary to God's love, and (4) it is repugnant to justice (see ibid. pg. 99)."**

* * * *

Is Christianity's teaching on eternal punishment "wholly unscriptural?" A relatively common accusation, as I witnessed house-to-house, was: "You people don't believe in hell." My response, "We do believe in hell but it's not a place of consciousness; it's the common grave of mankind. It can't be a place of torment because the Bible says the dead are unconscious, they're sleeping."

My next step was to "prove" my point from scripture. To the householder I would say, "Look here in the Bible, in Ecclesiastes 9:5, "For the living know that they will die but the dead know nothing; they have no further reward, even the memory of them is forgotten" (italics mine). Jehovah's Witnesses avoided the sixteen or so references the Lord Jesus made to after-life punishment of unbelievers. One such reference, "And if your eye causes you to sin, pluck it out. It is better for you to enter the kingdom of God with one eye than to be thrown into hell, where 'their worm does not die, and the fire is not quenched'" (see Mark 9:47,48). Another, "The Son of Man will send out his angels, and they will weed out of his kingdom everything that causes sin and all who do evil. They will throw them into the fiery furnace, where there will be weeping and gnashing of teeth" (see Matthew 13:41,42).

Also, some Old Testament verses support the doctrine of a literal conscious hell. "Multitudes who sleep in the dust of the earth will awake: some to everlasting life, others to shame and *everlasting contempt*" (see Daniel 12:2, Italics mine).

So, does the Bible contradict itself? Jesus often spoke of a literal hell where the souls of the unbelieving dead dwell, whereas Solomon wrote in Ecclesiastes "the dead know nothing."

As a Jehovah's Witness, I was accused of taking Bible verses out of context. I now realize that accusation was correct. The Ecclesiastes verse that follows the one I so often quoted continues, "... never again will they [the dead] have a part in anything that happens under the sun" (see Ecclesiastes 9:6). I would never have read this verse to a householder; it contradicts the Witness teaching that many of the dead will be bodily resurrected to live "under the sun," on a paradise earth. Why would the Watchtower Society pick one verse as foundational to their doctrine and dare not mention the next verse which seems to disprove another Witness doctrine? And why would they ignore the entire New Testament's body of evidence on hell?

Christian scholars never use Ecclesiastes as a foundation for doctrine. "The reason this book seems to clash with the rest of the Word of God is that it presents merely human reasoning 'under the sun,'" writes William MacDonald (see Believer's Bible Commentary - Old Testament volume pg. 875 © 1992 William Mac-Donald).

MacDonald continues, "This verse is constantly used by false teachers to prove that the soul sleeps in death, that consciousness ceases when the last breath is taken. But it is senseless to build a doctrine of the hereafter on this verse, or on this book, for that matter. As has been repeatedly emphasized, Ecclesiastes represents man's best conclusions as he searches for answers 'under the sun.' It sets forth deductions based on observations and logic but not on divine revelation." (see ibid pg. 907)

So, while Solomon's inspired writings in Ecclesiastes sometimes represent unspiritual thinking, they are valuable. They serve to remind us of the futility of negative thinking and actions. Solomon concludes the book with wise counsel, "... here is the conclusion of the matter: Fear God and keep his commandments, for this is the whole duty of man. For God will bring every deed into judgment, including every hidden thing, whether it is good or evil." (see Ecclesiastes 12:13,14)

The body of evidence from the Bible is irrefutable, the doctrine of a literal hell is supported by manifold scripture, it has been accepted by Christians since the time of Christ. It was taught by conservative Jewish scholars before Christ (see Antiquities of the Jews, Josephus Book XVIII, chap. I, par. 3 and Wars of the Jews, Josephus Book II, chap. VIII, par. 14). Jesus did not dispute Jewish beliefs in Hell, rather he contended with their leaders over their "adherence to tradition" (see Aid to Bible Understanding, Watchtower publication, 1971, pg. 1301, pars. 3,5).

* * * *

Of Watchtower founder C.T. Russell, the Witnesses write, "Brother Russell was well-aware that most sensible people did not really believe the doctrine of hellfire (see Watchtower book, Jehovah's Witnesses Proclaimers of God's Kingdom, pg. 129, © 1993)."

Russell lived at a time when 19th century theologians were advancing liberal theology. That is, if the ages old teachings of Christianity could not be scientifically proven they were considered irrational or superstitious. The Bible's miracles were denied, the deity of Christ rejected, the meaning of hell reinterpreted.

Russell adopted some of liberalism's tenets, rejecting the deity of Christ, denying the Trinity, and relegating the Holy Spirit to non-deity. His followers jokingly claimed that Russell had "put the hose on hell." Russell discarded the doctrines of the deity of Christ and the Holy Trinity, because he rejected them as incomprehensible, therefore false. **He likewise chose to reject the Christian doctrine of hell thinking it too was unreasonable.**

The fundamentalist movement (1910-current) attempted to counter religious liberalism and encouraged Christians to maintain their hold on the fundamentals of the faith. Jehovah's Witnesses are sometimes called "fundamentalists," but that is entirely wrong, they reject most of Christianity's key doctrines. They are not fundamentalists. They have accepted liberal religion's basic theological beliefs, rejecting: The deity of Christ, the Holy Trinity, the immortality of the soul, and the judgment of unbelievers in a conscious hell.

Recently I asked my therapist son, Bill, if controversial electric shock treatments were still used. He responded, "Yes, while no one actually understands how the electric shock changes behavior, it's relatively effective as a last resort for severely depressed patients." The lesson I took away from our conversation, just because something cannot be explained does not mean it cannot be true. I believe in the doctrine of hell because Jesus taught it. Its legitimacy is not dependent upon my feelings about it.

* * * *

Sometimes a householder would quote multiple scriptural proofs on the reality of hell. Unable to refute, I would quickly sidestep their proofs to change the argument. "How could a God of love torture his children in a literal hell?"

The thought of a punishing parent holding a disobedient child's hand on a red-hot stove was my favorite word-picture. But now in rebuttal of my former beliefs, I must point out that nowhere does the Bible say God punishes *his* children in hell. The Bible says all who place their faith in Jesus Christ become "children of God." "... To those who believed in His [Jesus] name, He gave the right to become children of God – children born not of natural descent, nor of human decision or of a husband's will, but born of God" (John 1:12,13). On the other hand, "Whoever believes in the Son has eternal life, but whoever rejects the Son will not see life, for *God's wrath remains on him*" (John 3:36, italics mine). "Children of God" are never punished in hell by God, they possess eternal life with Christ when they believe.

"Okay, so God doesn't punish *his* children in hell, **how could a God of love punish anyone eternally?**" I used to ask householders. But now I ask, "Does a loving God force people to love him?" And, "Does any person who truly loves another, coerce that person to respond in love?"

Furthermore, what about people, such as indigenous tribes, who have never been exposed to Jesus? Will a God of love give them an opportunity to be saved or will they go to hell? Jehovah's Witnesses

152

solve this problem by saying that most (except evil people like apostates) who die before Armageddon will be resurrected and have a second chance to accept their message, unless they are directly destroyed by Jehovah in the near future (Armageddon). Their teaching has appeal but cannot be supported by scripture.

Christian scholars teach that God uses "general" revelation to appeal to all peoples including those who have never heard the name, Jesus. General revelation refers to God's awe-inspiring creation, humans, animals, sun, moon, stars, mountains, rivers, lakes, and the like. Scholars cite the order demonstrated in creation as a part of God's general revelation and man himself, with his conscience, moral capabilities and intelligence. Further man, being "made in the image of God," has the ability to love, and the desire to worship. These attributes of man are considered part of God's general revelation.

Paul writes in Romans 1:20, "For since creation of the world God's invisible qualities – his eternal power and divine nature – have been clearly seen, being understood from what has been made, so that men are without excuse." Paul continued to explain that people rejected what can be known of God through his creation. Instead of acknowledging a Supreme Being they made idols. Worshipping what they could see, denying the spiritual.

Biblical scholar Charles Ryrie writes, "Man is justly condemned because he does not receive what God does tell him about Himself through Creation." (*Basic Theology*, Charles C. Ryrie, pg. 34) "If men do not make that minimal but crucial acknowledgement [that creation itself testifies of God], but rather turn away and offer some other explanation, then God is just if He rejects them and does not offer them any more truth." (Ibid. pgs. 37, 38)

Christian scholars believe that God, in his perfect love and total justice, will "offer more truth" to people who do not reject His power and divine nature as seen in creation. God will ultimately reveal the person of Jesus to isolated peoples who seek to know more of him.

Ryrie continues, "We must not forget that the majority of people who have ever lived have rejected the revelation of God through nature, and that rejection has come with scorn and deliberate substitution of their own gods. They have condemned themselves, and God rejects them, He does so justly." (ibid., pg. 38)

God-given freewill, to choose God or not, allows those who love him to be with him forever. That same freewill must also allow, those choosing not to love him, not to be with him. They choose eternal separation from God. Hell is their choice (see *Systematic Theology*, Vol. 4 Dr. Norman Geisler, Chapter 10).

* * * *

St. Augustine (AD 354-430) writes at length defending the reality of hell. Concerning God's justice in allowing the sin of unbelief and mankind's prerogative to choose hell, he reasoned that in society, crimes punished by the longest prison sentences were committed in the shortest possible time. No one ever suggests, Augustine argues, that the punishment of an offense should to be limited to the amount of time it took to commit the crime. Rather it is the magnitude of the act that is considered when meting out punishment (see *City of God Book* XXI, Chapters 11,12).

For example, it takes two minutes to rob a bank, should the bank robber be punished for only two minutes? The bandit receives ten or fifteen years in prison. Is his punishment disproportionate to his crime? No, the judge pronounces a sentence according to the magnitude of the crime.

Would it be just to punish Adolf Hitler with the same sentence as a "good" person who lived their life their own way; not harming others, but still rejecting Christ as the way to salvation, dying in unbelief? Jehovah's Witnesses believe so. Hitler will receive the identical punishment as "good" people who refuse to accept the truth as explained by their organization and are destroyed by God at Armageddon. The punishment, they believe, is eternal sleep (annihilation). Surely Roman governor Felix didn't "tremble" in fear of the prospect of eternal sleep as Paul detailed the "judgment to come." The details of unbeliever's judgment filled Felix with apprehension (see 2 Thessalonians 1:8,9; Revelation 21:8).

God is holy, pure beyond our comprehension. Isaiah saw the Lord, sitting on his throne, highly exalted, being worshipped by angels, "... calling to one another: Holy, holy, holy is the LORD God Almighty; the whole earth is full of his glory."

Isaiah immediately cried, "Woe is me! I am ruined. ... my eyes have seen the King, the LORD Almighty." (see Isaiah 6:1-6)

Upon Isaiah's conviction and confession of his personal sinfulness, God took his sin and guilt away. He purged him and ordained him as a prophet to Israel (Isaiah 6:7).

All sin, no matter how small or how great, grieves a Holy God. Sin separates us from God. God in his love and mercy has offered an infinite sacrifice for our sin, the death of his Son Jesus Christ on the cross. God invites everyone and forces no one to trust in the merit of Christ's ransom paid for all who believe. The problem is most of us do not want to admit we're sinners, but God says, "This righteousness from God comes through faith in Jesus Christ to all who believe ... *all have sinned* and fall short of the glory of God and are freely justified by his grace through the redemption that came by Christ Jesus." (see Romans 6:22-25, italics added)

God offers a perfect remedy for sin, those who refuse to be saved by that remedy commit the grave sin described in John 3:36. "... Whoever rejects the Son will not see life, for God's wrath remains upon him." The sin, of rejecting Christ is punishable by God's eternal wrath.

The God of Christianity is perfectly just whereas the "God" of Jehovah's Witnesses lacks perfect justice, he rewards all unbelievers equally regardless of their notoriety.

* * * *

My thoughts returned to the present and my exploration of the Holy Land. Paul's stay here in Caesarea must have been uncomfortable to say the least. Confined to the dungeon in the palace cellar, it was a dark, damp, physically demanding experience. But what a pleasant sight to behold today! Men casting their lines into the warm Mediterranean breeze, standing on palace ruins, unaware of the great Apostle's stint on that very outcropping.

Our Holy Land tour moves on, leaving the ruins of Caesarea's palace behind, the scene where Paul's gospel preaching left the Governor in holy terror. I wonder if Felix ever believed, one day we will know.

Chapter 19
A Complete Savior

"Therefore he [Jesus] is able to save completely those who come to God through him..." Hebrews 7:25

Back in the U.S., Custom's lines stretched for what seemed like a mile. I wondered whether we would ever make our connecting flight to Virginia. We should not be of much interest to Customs agents. Our Holy Land purchases were negligible and Roselie and I were not smuggling diamonds, drugs, or fresh Israeli fruit into the US. They should let us through without delay.

Finally, we arrived at the little stall, the official glanced at our passport, flicking through the visa pages, observed our just-finished travels, and he smiled. "Did you get to see the ancient church unearthed at Megiddo? They think it's the oldest church ever discovered?"

I replied, "Actually we were touring ancient Megiddo the same day they discovered it, but we didn't know about it until later. We saw it on the news in Jerusalem."

The inquiring officer again smiled, waving us by and bidding us "Good day."

Upon arriving home, I researched the Megiddo discovery.

The church was unearthed on November 6, 2005, is not amongst Megiddo's ancient ruins, but a few miles down the highway in the modern town. Construction workers were expanding a maximum-security prison. Excavations uncovered the remains of a church.

Israeli archaeologists dated the church as third century based on pottery shards, style of mosaic floor inlays, and Christian symbolism used. These evidences indicated a pre-Constantine (AD 312) meeting place.

The striking floor mosaic was extremely well preserved. The inscription: "The God-loving Acetous [Christianized Roman soldier] has offered this table to the God Jesus Christ as a memorial."[16]

My Christian view of Jesus' deity is in complete agreement with the Megiddo discovery – extolling Jesus Christ as God. More importantly the last Bible writer's gospel is affirmed by the archaeological finding. The apostle John (writing circa AD 90) wrote: "In the beginning was the Word, and the Word was with God, and *the Word was God*" (see John 1:1, italics added). Who is the "Word?" Everyone agrees – Jesus is the "Word" (see John 1:14).

Biblical scholars have concluded from their studies that Jesus is God. He is deity. Not surprisingly third century Christians worshipped Jesus as God as indicated by the inscription found in the Megiddo church.

The scholarly Pharisees of Jesus' day, understood his claim to Godhood. "... the Jews tried all the harder to kill him... he was even calling God his own Father, making himself equal to God" (see John 5:18).

On another occasion, again in Jerusalem, Jesus said, "I and the Father are one." "Again, the Jews picked up stones to stone him... 'for blasphemy,

---

[16] See www.washingtonpost.com, article, *Site may be 3rd-Century Place of Christian Worship*, Scott Wilson, Nov. 7, 2005.

because you, a mere man, claim to be God'" (see John 10:30-33).

Why is the deity (Godhood) of the Lord Jesus Christ foundational to Christianity? Early Biblical scholar Athanasius (293–373) for whom we credit the assemblage of the authorized New Testament books, taught that without a Savior who is fully God there could be no redemption of mankind. In other words, if Jesus was less than God, we could never be fully forgiven of all our sins, no hope of salvation (see *Encyclopedia Britannica*, 1978 edition, pg. 486).

I do not believe any other Christian doctrine has been dismissed or ridiculed as much as the deity of Christ and subsequently the doctrine of the Trinity (see chapter 14). Islam and Judaism have long accused Christians of polytheism, worshipping three Gods. Rationalistic secular and religious movements have rejected the doctrines as unexplainable, therefore improbable. All pseudo-Christian cults reject these doctrines, preferring to define Jesus according to their own imaginings. Author Dan Brown in his popular *Da Vinci Code* purports political reasons for the origin of these doctrines.

Pastor Charles Russell (1853–1916) founder of the Watchtower Society, likewise rejected the Christian doctrine of the Trinity. He viewed it as illogical, unscriptural, and of pagan origin.

Regarding John 1:1, the Witnesses state in one of their biographical sketches of Russell: "Other apologists for the Trinity appealed to John 1:1, but the Watch Tower analyzed that scripture based on both content and context to show that this in no way supported the Trinity."[17]

The Witness book I have just cited gives no explanation for the Watch Tower analysis which supposedly disproves John 1:1, as a scripture supportive of the Trinity. To the contrary nearly all Bible scholars cite John 1:1 as a critical text in support of the deity of Christ and the Trinity as fundamental doctrines of the Christian faith.

So, because the deity of Christ and the Trinity didn't seem logical, understandable and scriptural, to the founder of Jehovah's Witnesses, the doctrine was totally discarded.[18] When a religious body, claiming to be Christian, rejects the most fundamental of all Christian teachings, there will inevitably be conflict among that religion's adherents.

From my experience as a Jehovah's Witness, people would sometimes accuse us Witnesses of displaying a "holier-than-thou" attitude. I can honestly say that I did not feel sanctimonious or particularly pious. Yet in retrospect my thinking was indeed self-righteous, for I rationalized the holier-than-thou accusation in this way: People accused us because they felt guilty. They know they too should be out and about like me, telling people about their religion. God has given me the power to do this work. Other people lacked the power of God I had.

---

[17] *See Jehovah's Witnesses – Proclaimers of God's Kingdom, pg. 125, 126, published by the Watchtower Bible and Tract Society 1993.*
[18] *See Ibid, pg. 126.*

I believed I was more obedient to God than they, somehow spiritually superior. After all I was "in the truth" and they were led by the devil. Subconsciously I must have had a holier-than-thou attitude. It must have shown through in my everyday life. How does this observation relate to our discussion of Christ's deity and the Trinity doctrine? I'll explain shortly.

Now back to the Witnesses' rejection of Christ's deity and the Trinity.

Once again, fourth century church scholar Athanasius adamantly supported these doctrines because unless Jesus was fully God we humans could never be completely forgiven of sin. The redemption of sinful mankind could only be valid through the death of One who was fully God and yet fully human.[19]

By denying the deity of Christ, Jehovah's Witnesses must find a way to complete their salvation. The "Jesus" of the Watchtower organization cannot save completely, because he is not God. The created "Jesus" of Jehovah's Witnesses is only a partial savior; he did not pay the ransom price for all our sins, he could not pay it all (see Pg. 179, Appendix "Question and Answer" section – "Do Jehovah's Witnesses believe Jesus died for our sins?"). Unlike Jehovah's Witnesses, Christians believe Jesus was not a created being, rather he is God the Creator of all things (see John 1:3,4; Colossians 1:16,17). And unlike Jehovah's Witnesses, Christians worshipfully sing "Jesus paid it all, all to Him I owe; sin had left a crimson stain, He washed it

---

[19] *For a discussion on of the doctrine of the unity of deity and humanity of Jesus Christ – see Christian Theology Second Edition by Millard Erickson, 1999, pgs. 740, 741.*

white as snow." ("Jesus Paid It All;" *Baptist Hymnal*, 1956, Hall and Grape)

As a Jehovah's Witness, I believed our Jesus' death at Calvary could pay the price for only part of my sins. If I proved faithful by performing good works such as: spending time in house-to-house preaching, living an obedient life and faithfully attended Witness meetings, Jehovah God might allow me to survive Armageddon. Then at some future time I could become reconciled to God if I fully submitted to his reign over the paradise earth.

I believed in only partial forgiveness of sin. The Jesus of Jehovah's Witnesses could only pay for the sin I inherited from Adam. At some future time there existed the prospect of complete forgiveness or reconciliation, but always depending on my performance.[20]

Now back to the question, how does the rejection of these related fundamental Christian doctrines playout among Jehovah Witnesses? And what about the holier-than-thou accusation, how does that relate to the issue? I'm convinced my pious attitude, though unbeknownst to me at the time, was the result of my idolatry.

I believe because I had to depend on a "Jesus" who was only a partial savior and not Almighty God in the flesh, and then to add my own good deeds in order to be accepted by God, I was necessarily elevating myself to god-like status, that of co-savior. My

---

[20] See *Kingdom of the Cults*, 1997 edition pg. 152, Walter Martin, Bethany House.

unknowing efforts to assume deity were reflected in my "holier-than thou" attitude.

Bible scholar, Tim Keller, likens relying on self-goodness for salvation to idolatry as he comments on *Martin Luther's Treatise on Good Works* (1520). "Here Luther says failure to believe that God accepts us fully in Christ – and to look to something else for our salvation – is a failure to keep the first commandment; namely, having no other gods before him. To try to earn your own salvation through works-righteousness is breaking the first commandment. Then he [Luther] says that we cannot truly keep any of the other laws unless we keep the first law – against idolatry and works-righteousness. Thus, beneath any particular sin is the sin of rejecting Christ-salvation and indulging in self-salvation."[21]

I believe I was unknowingly living the promise of Satan's original lie, "...you will be like God..." (see Genesis 3:5). Rising to and ultimately attaining godhood is a consistent theme in eastern religious thought. It is adamantly rejected by conservative Jewish and Christian scholars.

English writer/columnist, G. K. Chesterton (1874–1936) once said "Abolish God and the government becomes God." In the case of Jehovah's Witnesses, they did not abolish God, but they did demote their Jesus down to the status of an incomplete savior, a "god." Then they elevated their Governing Body to what I consider godlike status. We were

---

[21] *Talking About Idolatry in a Postmodern Age*, Tim Keller, source: The Gospel Coalition http://www.monergism.com/postmodernidols.html

admonished to "stick close to the "organization"." We should have been admonished to stick close to Jesus rather than any human organization. No society or organization has the power to save. When the Society issued new light, I was quick to obey without question. I would never have spoken negatively of "God's organization," even though their directives sometimes violated my conscience. I believed any hope for everlasting life would vanish if I was disrespectful of "God's organization." Not all family members or friends were as devout as me. I was always disturbed to hear about loved ones expressing disagreement over Witness teachings. Sometimes one would dare to downplay the governing body as "a bunch of old men," out of touch with reality.

If sticking close to the organization required laying down my life, I was ready. In the name of Jehovah, I would defend my Society leaders and their proclamations at any cost.

I am grateful to have met the Jesus of the Bible. My futile attempts at self-salvation, religious idolatry, have been forgiven.

* * * *

Jehovah's Witnesses surely explain the Megiddo archeological find as an instance of idolatry. An altar inscription with the words "... to the God Jesus Christ..." is to Witnesses blasphemous and idolatrous.

Now on return trips to the Holy Land, I declare to fellow travelers, "Look out the window on your right. You are seeing the Megiddo prison, an Israeli maximum-security facility holding 1,200 inmates. Back in November 2005, preparing for expansion, excavation workers uncovered what may be the oldest church ever found. The discovery here at Megiddo remains closed to the public but it is being preserved by the government. The beautiful floor mosaic reads, 'The God loving Acetous has offered this table to the God Jesus Christ as a memorial.'"

The early church recognized the deity of Christ. Members believed he was a complete Savior, therefore One that could save without added works of righteousness.

Chapter 20
Conclusion

Thank you for reading my life's story and observations.

I was once a worried child striving to obey seemingly infinite Watchtower rules. I transitioned into joyless leadership in Jehovah's Witnesses. And finally, unimaginably – transforming into a follower of "My Lord and my God," Jesus Christ (see John 20:28). Because of my rebirth in Christ, I was disfellowshipped, banished from the Witnesses, disowned by friends and family. Yet my life today overflows with God's blessings.

My story, beginning in the 1950's continues in this second decade of the 21st century. Like the old church hymn resounds, "I Love to Tell the Story," the joy of my heart is to tell the story of my dearest friend, Jesus. By God's providence, I have walked in HIS footsteps through Galilee. In Jerusalem, I have retraced the path of HIS sorrow to the cross. I have meditated alongside the tomb from which HE victoriously arose to glory.

I have just returned from my fifth Holy Land pilgrimage. My thirst for intimacy with Jesus is unquenchable. My heart's desire is that I will allow nothing to captivate my heart except the name of Jesus.

A few departing thoughts…

First, I hope and pray for a thorough reformation within Jehovah's Witnesses, a revolution, resulting in organizational acceptance of the orthodox beliefs of Christianity. I believe that with God, all things are possible. But how can one relate, on an individual level, to family, friends and workmates professing to be Jehovah's Witnesses?

To Christians, if it is your heart's desire to share the gospel of Jesus with Jehovah's Witnesses, remember that in contrast with the simple Christian gospel, the Watchtower's path-to-life is quite complex. I would not encourage anyone to invest multitudinous hours trying to learn all the doctrinal tenants of the Witnesses. Witnesses study hard, preparing to rebut objections to their doctrines; they earnestly await you. Rather, I contend, simply tell them the true gospel – believe on the Lord Jesus Christ and be saved.

Do your Witness friends seem to have a conviction of their sins? Do they know they are unable to save themselves from their transgressions? If your Jehovah's Witness friends have a sense of being lost, why not ask them if they would like to hear your story? Explain that you once were lost, separated from God because of your sins. Tell them that Jesus loved you so much he was willing to die on a cruel cross as payment for your sins and you received Jesus in faith, asking Him to forgive and save you. Be prepared to share appropriate gospel scriptures along with your testimony (For example: Romans 3:23; 6:23; 5:8; 10:10,13). No extensive study or special knowledge is required. Yield to God and ask to be guided by His Holy Spirit.

The simple truth of the gospel coupled with the power of God's Spirit and love for our neighbor is sufficient. We do not need to be prepared to debate the validity of their complex doctrines. Seemingly, to Witnesses that which is not logical cannot be true. Remember your message is not humanly logical anyway. How could one man die for the sins of all mankind? How can a person be saved by simply believing in that person? The love of Christ defies human logic. Yet we know it is true, because we have been set free. It is promised in His word, "You shall know the truth and the truth shall set you free."

The hard-fact is: though the gospel is simple, it can be difficult to accept. How hard it is for a person to admit they are in error, ask for forgiveness of their transgressions, believe the simple good news, and be set free. If your Jehovah's Witness friend is not receptive do not force it on him or her. You can plant seeds and water them with the Word of God, but only God can make them grow.

Can your Jehovah's Witness acquaintances sense your heartfelt love for them? They will if you are praying for them.

Of course, we want them to be set free from religious bondage, but our agenda should be not hidden. Tell them you wish they could be as you, forgiven. If they reject your offer you must continue to love them just as Jesus commanded – "love your neighbor as yourself." (Matthew 22:38-40)

Second, to those trapped in any oppressive religious system, take heart. You can leave. Jesus will take care of you. One of my favorite Bible verses are the powerful words of David in Psalm 27:10, "Though my mother and father forsake me, the LORD will receive me." The power of this verse has brought blessed comfort to me, and to the weeping young man I met at Jerusalem's Garden Tomb (see Chapter 12), I've used it to encourage others in similar trials of rejection.

From experience, I know it is possible to live an abundant life, even when severed from one's natural family and life-long friends. I know that life can be filled with joy, peace, and God's glory.

Some religious systems threaten torture, imprisonment, or even death upon one's conversion to Jesus. Christ alone can forgive your sins; no man can do that. Christ alone can set you free. No man can do that. Christ alone grants eternal life to those who believe in Him. I am convinced that following Jesus is worth any price demanded by earthly authorities, religious or secular.

To Jehovah's Witnesses, please don't ask your children to take a position on issues you yourself are unwilling to face. I'm certainly not suggesting children be allowed to do everything the culture demands. But if many Watchtower regulations are in fact unbiblical commands of men, rather than from God, expect to damage your child by requiring his obedience to those rules. But if such are from God, God will empower the child with His Holy Spirit, like the three Hebrew boys who refused to worship King Nebuchadnezzar's golden image. They prospered and suffered no mental or emotional damage, only blessings of God.

So, Witness parents have mercy on your children. The kindest thing you can do, I believe, is to encourage your child to seek the truth. Paul commended the church in Berea, "Now the Bereans were of more noble character than the Thessalonians, for they received the message with great eagerness and examined the Scriptures every day to see if what Paul said was true" (Acts 17:11).

And to teachers, love your students. As a child, the kindest words I ever heard from a teacher were, "Dwight, I don't agree with your religion, but I still love you anyway."

Finally, to everyone who is wearied and sin-burdened – Jesus invites you: "Come to me, all you are weary and burdened, and I will give you rest. Take My yoke upon you and learn from Me, for I am gentle and humble in heart, and you will find rest for your souls. For My yoke is easy and My burden is light" (Matthew 11:28-30).

Part 3

Questions and Answers

For thirty years, people have asked me questions about Jehovah's Witnesses. Here are my answers to some of those questions.

Q. How many Jehovah's Witnesses are there?

A. At the time of this writing (2010), there are approximately eight million worldwide. However, their influence is exponentially greater. The Watchtower magazine is the most widely published periodical in the world. It has a distribution of about eighty million copies per month in 182 languages. The Awake! A companion magazine to the Watchtower has a circulation of about seventy-six million copies each month. The Witnesses also distribute millions of tracts, booklets, books. Their Bible, The New World Translation of the Holy Scriptures, has had a printing of 165 million copies in 83 languages.

Millions of people are sympathetic to some beliefs of Jehovah's Witnesses but are not interested in being identified with them, accepting every doctrine they expound. These people reject the difficult teachings like refusing blood transfusions but covertly accept the pleasing doctrines like the absence of a literal hell.

Q. Are Jehovah's Witnesses just another Christian denomination?

A. No, the Witnesses are radical separatists. They believe all Christendom is condemned and unless the churches make a drastic change and follow Watchtower teachings they are doomed for destruction.

They do not want to be viewed as Protestant.

They believe that their founder Pastor C.T. Russell (1852-1916) was used by God to restore the true Christian faith to which they alone adhere. They reject nearly all the basic beliefs of orthodox Christianity.

They fail to meet the principal criteria for acceptance into the National Council of Churches – belief in the Incarnation – Almighty God coming in the flesh in the person of Jesus Christ. (see John 1:1,14)

Q. Do Jehovah's Witnesses believe that the restoration of modern Israel fulfills Bible prophecy?

A. No, not today, although earlier Witnesses did. Founder Russell expounded dispensational (end times prophecy) teachings the same as many Christians. Some historians consider Russell to be pro-Zionist. Later Watchtower president Rutherford denounced that view. In 1932 the witnesses rejected any connection between the re-gathering of modern Israel and Bible prophecy. (Let God be True, 2nd ed., pages. 217, 218)

Watchtower President Rutherford (1869-1942) claimed that Jewish leaders were "arrogant, self-important and extremely selfish" (see Favored People, Watchtower publication, pg. 129). About that same time he annulled the teaching that modern Israel has a role in the fulfillment of Bible prophecy.

Q. Do Jehovah's Witnesses believe in Jesus Christ?

A. This was one of the most commonly asked questions. Jehovah's Witnesses do not believe in the historic Christ of the Bible. Their "Jesus" is not the divine Creator of all (see John 1:3; Colossians 1: 16,17) but rather part of the creation. He is described by Jehovah's Witnesses as "a god." Paul warned against the preaching of "another Jesus." The Jesus of the Witnesses is a different Jesus from that of historical Christianity (see 2 Corinthians 11:4 KJV).

Q. Do Jehovah's Witnesses accept the Bible as their authority?

A. Jehovah's Witnesses teach that the Bible is from God and is inspired by God. They are taught to hold the Bible in high regard. They urge people to read the Bible. They say that the Bible holds the answer to all life's problems. But they do not believe a person can discover the "truth" using the Bible alone apart from the Watchtower Society and its publications.

Jehovah's Witnesses are taught that biased Bible translators have slanted the Scriptures to reflect their "false" Trinitarian views.

Witnesses teach that the Bible is their ultimate authority. But adherents must follow the current scripture interpretations dispensed by the Watchtower Society. In my view the Watchtower Society is the final authority for Jehovah's Witnesses, not the Bible.

Their *New World Translation* of the Bible is used at their meetings and in their door-to-door preaching.

Q. Did Jehovah's Witnesses preach that the world would end in 1914?

A. Through the history of the Watchtower Society, the Witnesses have set several end-time dates. Their cardinal date, 1914 AD, figured prominently in Watchtower dogma. Originally it was predicted that all worldly kingdoms would end in 1914. As years went by, the meaning of 1914 has been redefined. Obviously, the governments of the world survived 1914. The Society then clarified their failed prediction claiming that Jesus began his invisible reign over the earth in that year.

More recently the 1914 date has been reinterpreted as "a prophecy providentially causing sincere Bible students of the 19th century to be in expectation" (see Watchtower, Sept. 15, 1998, pg. 15). Evidently the year 1914 is of no real prophetic value. Predictions of a soon-coming end of the world's systems served to keep people focused on the urgency of the times, they claimed.

Q. Do Jehovah's Witnesses believe in the second coming of Christ?

A. Witnesses believe that their Jesus came invisibly to rule with kingly power in 1914. He has been ruling invisibly over the earth ever since. He will come invisibly to bring destruction to all nations at Armageddon and rule invisibly over the earth for a thousand years.

Q. Why do modern Watchtower publications rarely use the title "Lord" for Jesus, as in "the Lord Jesus Christ?"

A. The word "Lord" denotes a master or owner. The Bible uses this title repeatedly to honor the Lord Jesus. First Corinthians 12:3 teaches "... no one can say, 'Jesus is Lord,' except by the Holy Spirit." One must belong to Jesus if he is to address him as "Lord," and really mean it (see The Living Bible paraphrase, 1 Corinthians 12:3). Christian books and magazines call Jesus "Lord," identifying their writers as servants of Christ.

In the gospel accounts even demons could address Jesus as "Son of the Most High God." But they could never address him as "Lord" because he was not their "Master." Their Lord, master and owner was Satan (see Mark 1:24; 5:7).

Non-Christians will not refer to Jesus as their "Lord."

Look through a current issue of the Watchtower magazine, count how many times you see the phrase, "the Lord Jesus Christ." Almost always he is addressed with no title or as "God's Son." Almost never is he called "Lord" except in direct scripture quotes.

Secular historians as well as Jehovah's Witnesses prefer to use the B.C.E. (before common era) and C.E. (common era) dating system. By avoiding A.D. (anno Domini - "in the year of the Lord," one avoids acknowledging Jesus as Lord. By avoiding B.C. one avoids acknowledging Jesus as Christ at his birth. Jehovah's Witnesses do not believe Jesus was Christ at birth (see Luke 2:26).

Q. Do Jehovah's Witnesses believe that Jesus is the Son of God?

A. Yes, they answer. However they have an entirely different definition in mind from Christian thought. They believe, "... he was the first son that Jehovah God brought forth... He was the first of Jehovah's creations," (*Let God be True* 1952 pg.32). They believe their Jesus, was the first of many sons and that he was inferior to God because he himself was not divine, but rather created and thus a part of creation.

The Christian view of the Son of God is that Jesus is of the same nature as the Father. Both are divine; therefore both are God. "For this reason, the Jews tried all the harder to kill him; not only was he breaking the Sabbath, but he was even calling God his own Father, making himself equal with God" (see John 5:18). "In the beginning was the Word [Jesus], and the Word was with God, and the Word was God" (see John 1:1; brackets added, and also see John 1:14).

In all the universe there are only two kinds of beings, either Creator or created. All life fits into one category or the other. The Jesus of the Bible is creator of all things. The Jesus of Jehovah's Witnesses is a created being; he is not creator of all things. (see John 1:3)

Q. Do Jehovah's Witnesses believe in the Trinity?

A. No, they despise the very word "Trinity," Three Persons – one God. To Witnesses, it is idolatry to exalt Jesus to a divine being. Witnesses also reject the personality and deity of the Holy Spirit, considering him to be an "it," an impersonal force from God. The Watchtower's Bible translation, unlike other translations, refuses to capitalize the word "spirit" when referring to the Holy Spirit. Witnesses slant their translation to depersonalize the Holy Spirit in keeping with Watchtower theology.

Their Bible (*New World Translation*) translates John 1:1, "In the beginning the Word was, and the Word was with God, and *the Word was a god.*" (italics added)

The Apostle John was a Jew who believed that "the LORD our God is one LORD." It is difficult to imagine that he wrote down "a god" in the opening verse of his gospel. He would have been acknowledging another god in addition to the one true God (see Deuteronomy 6:4).

The namesake Bible text for Jehovah's Witnesses is Isaiah 43:10. It reads, "'YOU are my witnesses,' is the utterance of Jehovah, 'even my servant whom I have chosen, in order that YOU may know and have faith in, and that you may understand that I am the same One. *Before me there was no God formed and after me there continued to be none.* I–I am Jehovah, and besides me there is no savior.'" (Isaiah 43:10,11, *New World Translation*, Italics added) Christians believe in one God, not in a greater God and a lesser god duo as do the Jehovah's Witnesses.

Q. How do Jehovah's Witnesses view the spiritual sign gifts like miracles, speaking in tongues, and receiving a word of knowledge from God?

A. They follow the same principles outlined by fundamentalist B.B. Warfield in his book, *Miracles: Yesterday and Today*. Special sign gifts of the Holy Spirit, Witnesses claim, have all ceased. They teach these gifts are no longer needed.

Q. Why do Jehovah's Witnesses refuse to wear a cross?

A. Jehovah's Witnesses were allowed to honor the cross up until 1936, after which its use was forbidden. The Witness Bible even eliminated the word "cross" and translated it as "torture stake."

The Bible says, "For the preaching of the cross is to them that perish, foolishness; but unto us which are saved it is the power of God" (see 1 Corinthians 1:18 KJV). The power of the preaching of the cross is the message that the Lord Jesus loved us so much that he was willing to suffer and die as payment for our sins on that cruel instrument of execution.

Jehovah's Witnesses are not alone in forbidding their followers to use the cross. Other 19th century restorationist groups also refuse to allow the display of the cross on their buildings, books or be worn on person.

When confronted with the absence of the cross, the ubiquitous symbol of Christianity, Witnesses sometimes reply, "Well if a loved one died by gunshot, you wouldn't wear a little replica of a gun around your neck, would you?" Rather than address the Bible's value placed on the cross, the Witnesses are trained to offer a diversionary argument.

Q. Do Jehovah's Witnesses believe Jesus died for our sins?

A. The Watchtower Society teaches that their Jesus died for part of our sins, namely the sin inherited from Adam. "The perfect human life which Jesus laid down in death is that valuable thing which accomplishes the purchase of what Adam's sin of disobedience lost for all his offspring" (see Let God be True, 1952, pg. 116). But the Bible teaches that the Lord Jesus is the "Lamb of God that takes away the sin of the world" (John 1:29). He is the payment for all sin, not just Adam's inherited sin.

Q. Do Jehovah's Witnesses believe Jesus is their Mediator?

A. The Watchtower organization teaches that Jesus is Mediator "solely" for the 144,000. He is not the Mediator for the larger body of more than eight million Jehovah's Witnesses. (See Watchtower publication, Aid to Bible Understanding, 1971 edition, pg. 1130.)

Q. Do Jehovah's Witnesses believe in the bodily resurrection of Jesus?

A. No, they teach that his body was not resurrected. God hid or dissolved it so it was missing from the tomb. God then raised Jesus to eternal life as a "glorious spirit creature." (Ibid. pg. 276) They believe Jesus "materialized" into different bodily forms as he appeared to his disciples following his resurrection.

The Christian view differs. According to it Jesus was raised in a glorified human body, not as a ghost or spirit. He said to the disciples, "Look at my hands and my feet. It is I myself! Touch me and see; a ghost does not have flesh and bones, as you see I have." (Luke 24:39) Three years earlier he had spoken of his resurrected body, "Jesus answered them, 'Destroy this temple, and I will raise it again in three days.'" "But the temple He had spoke of was H*is body*" (John 2:19,21, italics mine).

Q. Why do Christians not use the name "Jehovah" as often as Jehovah's Witnesses?

A. Jehovah's Witnesses believe they honor the Heavenly Father by recognizing and using his personal name. They believe that the churches are trying to hide God's name from people. They say that it is the Witnesses purpose to make that name known throughout the whole earth, thus their name "Jehovah's Witnesses."

Actually the name "Jehovah" is more used by Christians than Witnesses realize, particularly in Christian music. Since the actual pronunciation of the divine name has been lost over the centuries, some scholars prefer to use the form "Yahweh," believing it closer to the original, but unknown, Hebrew pronunciation. The English form "Jehovah" was apparently of medieval construction.

Christians have no problem addressing God with his titles "God" or "Lord."

Most children do not address their parents by their first names. They use titles such as Mom or Dad, not their personal names. People would be even less likely to address a parent using a personal name if they were uncertain as to how the name was pronounced. When addressed by a respectful title, "Mom," "Dad," "Grandma," "Grandpa," a person's heart is warmed. My wife's name is Roselie, almost no one pronounces it in two syllables as it is written, most call her Rosalie, Roselle, Rosalind or a dozen other names. She responds warmly when I call her "Honey." Our children call her

"Mom." Grandchildren call her "Grandma Rose." Business associates call her "Mrs. Hayes." Her titles are more endearing to her than hearing her name mispronounced.

The real issue, however, is: who is Jehovah? Witnesses are taught that Jehovah is God the Father. They have assigned Jesus the role as "a god." They actually believe in a greater God, Jehovah, the Father, and in a lesser god, Jesus the Son. Their belief is contrary to the doctrines of both Jews and Christians, the belief in one God.

The Christian view is that Jehovah is the name of God. Therefore, the Father is Jehovah, Jesus is Jehovah and the Holy Spirit is Jehovah – three persons, one God.

Just two of many proofs that Jesus is Jehovah in the Scriptures: "Before me [Jehovah] every knee will bow." (Isaiah 45:23b) and Paul writes "That at the name of Jesus every knee should bow, in heaven and on earth and under the earth, and every tongue confess that Jesus Christ is Lord, to the glory of God the Father" (Philippians 2:10,11). Paul obviously had in mind Jehovah's words as he quotes Isaiah, he identified the New Testament Lord Jesus as the Old Testament Jehovah.

Secondly; in John 12:41, the Apostle John writes, "Isaiah said this because *he saw Jesus' glory* and spoke about him" (Italics added). How did the prophet Isaiah see "Jesus' glory?"

Isaiah saw Jehovah the God of Israel -- "... and my eyes have seen the King, the LORD Almighty" (Isaiah 6:5). Later Isaiah "spoke about him [Jesus]." He said, "But he was pierced for our transgressions, he was crushed for our iniquities; the punishment that brought us peace was upon him, and by his wounds we are healed" (Isaiah 53:5). Apostle John clearly identifies Jesus as Jehovah of the Old Testament.

Q. If only 144,000 Jehovah's Witnesses go to heaven, what about the other eight million, aren't they disappointed they'll never see Jesus, spending eternity with him?

A. No disappointment at all. When you are personally acquainted with someone, you long to see that person. When someone is a stranger to you there is little desire to be with them. The average Jehovah's Witness did not claim to have a personal relationship with the Lord Jesus Christ. Without that, they lacked any desire to be with Jesus, to talk to him, to worship him, and spend eternity with him.

Witnesses are taught if faithful to God and his organization they can gain life on a paradise earth. The mind can imagine plenty of earthly things to occupy an eternity on earth. Perhaps, gardening, farming, creating art from scenes on this beautiful earth, just to name a few of our human desires to be fulfilled throughout everlasting earthly life.

When one becomes a believer in Jesus: one knows him, loves him and wants to be with him, one wants to talk to him and worship him as God. Jesus said, "If you love me, you will obey what I command. And I will ask the Father, and he will give you another Counselor to be with you forever – the Spirit of truth. The world cannot accept him, because it neither sees him, for he lives with you and will be in you" (see John 14:15- 17a). He promises the Holy Spirit will indwell those who love him.

Further Jesus promises, "If anyone loves me, he will obey my teaching. My Father will love him, and we will come to him and make our home with him." (John 14:23) Not only will the Holy Spirit dwell within the Christian believer, but Jesus says the Father and the Son will dwell in the believer. That makes three persons dwelling in a believer but one God dwelling in him.

Jehovah Witnesses say they love Jesus. But how can a person love Jesus when they are forbidden to communicate with him? In human relationships our love for another is communicated by words. Witnesses are not allowed to speak to Jesus; but the Bible cites examples of person speaking, in prayer, to Jesus (see Acts 7-59; 1 Timothy 1:12).

Q. Do Jehovah's Witnesses celebrate communion?

A. Once each year, on the night of the Jewish Passover, Jehovah's Witnesses assemble to observe the "Memorial," the remembrance of Christ's death. This special meeting is heavily promoted as an evangelistic outreach. About eighteen million people attended according to the latest figures.

As the bread and wine are passed only a few with the "call" to heavenly life partake. They number about ten thousand (those still remaining of the 144,000). Obviously most of the more than 100,000 congregations will have no one partaking at all. Eighteen million people will observe only as the bread and wine are passed in front of them; they must not partake.

Q. Do Jehovah's Witnesses meet on Saturday or Sunday?

A. Witnesses assemble at the Kingdom Hall for two contiguous meetings on Sunday. Where Kingdom Halls are shared by more than one congregation, the meeting times are scheduled accordingly. For example, if five congregations share the same Kingdom Hall building, some of the congregations may need to meet on Saturday.

Q. Do Jehovah's Witnesses baptize?

A. Yes, they follow the Baptist tradition of totally immersing persons, one time backwards. Only those old enough to understand the Witnesses' explanation of baptism are immersed.

They teach that baptism is a requirement, "... baptism is not to be viewed of little importance. It is a requirement for all who obediently walk in the footsteps of Jesus Christ" (see *The Truth That Leads To Eternal Life*, pg. 184) "Dedication and baptism are... essential for survival." (see Watchtower book, *Knowledge That Leads To Everlasting Life*, pg. 180)

In 1959 when I was baptized, the Witness who baptized me recited "I baptize you in the name of the Father and of the Son and of the Holy Ghost" (see Matthew 28:19,20). It is my understanding that Jehovah's Witnesses are now asked these two questions upon baptism.

1) "On the basis of the sacrifice of Jesus Christ, have you repented of your sins and dedicated yourself to Jehovah to do his will?

2) Do you understand that your dedication and baptism identify you as one of Jehovah's Witnesses in association with God's spirit-directed organization" (see The Watchtower, April 1, 2006, pgs. 21-25)?

Q. According to Jehovah's Witnesses, will the unrighteous dead be resurrected?

A. The Witnesses say that many of the unrighteous dead will not be resurrected. For example, notoriously wicked people and especially those who turn against "the truth" which is found exclusively within the Watchtower organization are annihilated forever.

The problem is that the Bible says in at least three places that all the wicked shall be resurrected to stand judgment (see Daniel 12:2; John 5:28,29; Acts 24:15).

Q. Do Jehovah's Witnesses believe in hell?

A. No, see Chapter 18 for a detailed explanation. Watchtower Society founder Charles T. Russell followed the thinking of mid-19th century liberal religionists in rejecting the doctrine of conscious punishment for the unbelieving. He also borrowed the Adventist notion of soul sleep. He taught that those in the grave were in a state of unconsciousness. At a future time, some would be resurrected to heavenly life (exactly 144,000) but the vast majority to life on earth. All resurrected to life on earth would receive a physical body and have their immaterial spirit restored to them from God's memory. Those resurrected to life on earth would have a second chance to obey God and receive everlasting life if obedient.

Russell's idea of a second-chance for most of mankind in some ways reflects liberal religion's drift towards universalism. While some churches taught that all mankind will be saved (universalism), Russell taught that most of dead mankind would have one more opportunity to obey God and prove worthy of life.

A second chance, according to the Bible, is not offered.

Jesus spoke simply: "Whoever believes in the Son has eternal life, but whosoever rejects the Son will not see life, for God's wrath remains upon him." (John 3:36)

Like many in liberal churches, Jehovah's Witnesses reason that the ages-old Christian doctrine of hell is unreasonable and unjust. However, Jesus clearly addressed the plight of unbelievers: "If your hand causes you to sin, cut it off. It is better for you to enter life maimed than with two hands to go into hell, where the fire never goes out." (Mark 9:44)

The doctrine of hell is not a feel-good subject, rather it is the unhappy consequence of those who reject Jesus as Lord and savior. "Whoever believes in him is not condemned, but whoever does not believe stands condemned already because he has not believed in the name of God's one and only Son (John 3:18)."

Q. Do Jehovah's Witnesses believe in doctors?

A. Yes, they accept all forms of medical treatment except for blood transfusions.

Q. Why do Jehovah Witnesses forbid blood transfusions?

A. Jehovah's Witnesses appeal to a number of Bible texts to support their ban on blood transfusions. The scriptures used (see Genesis 9:4; Leviticus 17:10; Acts 15:28,29) refer to a ban on eating blood for bodily nourishment. The Watchtower doctrine developed from a medical doctor's opinion that a blood transfusion feeds or nourishes the patient. So the Watchtower organization interpreted a transfusion as eating blood.

Despite the understanding that blood transfusions were wrong, it wasn't until 1961 that a Witness could be disfellowshipped for accepting a transfusion. If he repented of his wrong act (receiving the blood) he would perhaps be disciplined in a less severe manner.

The May 22, 1994 issue of the Society's Awake! magazine displayed pictures of more than two dozen children up to age 17; all refused blood transfusions. Some died for lack of a transfusion. All of them are extolled as heroes of their faith.

It is estimated that thousands of Witnesses, have died for lack of a blood transfusion. The Watchtower organization has pushed for newer technology for bloodless surgeries. Often patients that survive without blood transfusion make excellent physical recovery. Amazed doctors are quoted as suggesting that the patient's God has protected the patient in miraculous ways. The Witnesses consider this a "sign" that Jehovah has blessed their obedience.

While organ transplants were forbidden for a number of years, they are now again permitted by the Society.

It is my opinion that if the Watchtower Society were to reverse its stand on blood transfusions they would be immediately hit with thousands of lawsuits. Surviving family members, particularly non-Witnesses would, I believe, sue over the wrongful death of their loved ones, especially for those which it could be proven had died for lack of a transfusion. The Society has liberalized it blood policy again and again, for example now allowing formerly forbidden vaccinations, because the serums were derived from blood products. I would not be surprised to see the Society attempt a complete phase out of the blood transfusion ban. I think they would attempt it over 30 or 40 years to diminish their legal liability.

Q. Are Jehovah's Witnesses allowed to defend their country?

A. No, they are not to engage in any military activity or noncombatant role for any government. During the era of the U.S. Selective Services draft young men were sometimes assigned Noncombatant Conscientious Objector status. The Watchtower discouraged them from accepting any alternative service such as working in a V.A. hospital.

If a young Witness man "compromised" by accepting a noncombatant job, he was not to be disfellowshipped but rather "disassociated" for his error. Disassociation, while essentially the same as disfellowshipping, I understood was said to be used so the government would not trouble the Witnesses.

Jehovah's Witnesses do not consider themselves pacifists. They believe in war, God's war, Christ is about to bring a war against this world, the ultimate battle, Armageddon. They decline military service on the basic of John 18:36, "My [Jesus] kingdom is not part of this world ..." They believe being neutral towards the world includes not fighting its wars, voting, nor any political involvement.

Q. Why do Jehovah's Witnesses refuse to celebrate birthdays and holidays?

A. They believe too much honor is given to an individual by observing birthdays. The Witnesses cite Biblical examples where a birthday turned tragic, such as John the Baptist being executed on Herod's Birthday (see Matthew 14:6-10).

However, they pay little attention to Jesus' birthday in Bethlehem where the angels celebrated and gifts were later presented. Interestingly, the Christ child's devout Jewish mother, Mary, and stepfather Joseph allowed the Wise Men to see and worship the child Jesus. Mary and Joseph, being godly Jews, would never allow their child to be worshipped, unless of course they understood their Child to be Immanuel, "God with us." (Matthew 1:23; 2:11)

Progressively over the years the Watchtower has banned birthdays and Christmas. At first, they celebrated them, then discouraged their celebration and finally made it a disfellowshipping offense to observe them.

Holidays are either from a pagan religious origin or they are from political decree, according to Jehovah's Witnesses. Pagan trappings of Christmas are cited as a major reason for the Witnesses' rejection of that holiday. However, Paul the Apostle wrote about the Christian believer's freedom, "Everything is permissible – but not everything is beneficial." (1 Corinthians 10:23) Paul taught that it was permissible to eat meat sacrificed in pagan temples. Christians eating meat sacrificed to idols did not think of themselves as worshipping pagan deities. Christians celebrating Christ's birth do not regard Christmas decorations as symbols of pagan deities.

Witnesses do practice cremation of the dead, a pagan practice. They do wear wedding rings, a pagan practice. They drive cars named after pagan gods such as Saturn or Mercury. They utter and write the pagan - names of the days, Sunday (Sun god), Monday (Moon god), etc.

Mother's Day and Father's Day are also considered wrong by Witnesses because those days honor humans rather than God. But the Bible teaches, "Honor your father and mother which is the first commandment with a promise." (Ephesians 6:2)

All patriotic holidays honor the political nation from which Jehovah's Witnesses stay separate. Even Thanksgiving Day was established by a political leader therefore Witnesses must abstain in order to be "no part of this world."

The Watchtower organization allows observances of wedding anniversaries. Happily, many Witnesses have turned their anniversary into a gift-giving-time for all in order that their children can have one annual event on which to give and receive gifts.

Q. Should I give a Christmas or birthday gift to my Witness friend, relative, or employee?

A. Witnesses try to inform gift givers of their religious rules before accepting holiday gifts. They want to be certain that the giver understands that they are non-participants in all holidays.

Most Witnesses are delighted to receive a holiday gift. Christmas bonuses or a Thanksgiving turkey are also appreciated. But, they feel obligated to explain, "Thank you so much for your gift. But as you may know I don't celebrate Christmas (or Thanksgiving), but thank you for your generosity." Often an employer will graciously respond, "I want you to accept my gift, you need not think of it as a Christmas gift."

Q. As a school teacher, how should I relate to my Witness students?

A. Actually the children are not officially Jehovah's Witnesses until they are baptized. Nonetheless they are usually required to obey the tenets of their religion from infancy. I encourage teachers to be compassionate and unprejudiced with children from Witness homes.

I always liked the teachers who said, "Honey, I don't believe the same as you do, but I still love and respect you." Contrast that with a teacher who tried to force me to salute the flag or enjoyed embarrassing me or turned away when socially prominent kids were punching me, calling me a "communist."

I used to admire fellow students who had the fortitude to take a stand against the evolution theory in science class. They were born again Christians, while I disagreed with most of their beliefs, I did agree with their position against evolution, but I didn't have the power needed to take a strong stand, as they did. I now experience that same power, the power of the Holy Spirit.

Teacher, if the child's parents haven't talked to you about the multitude of things their child must not participate in, please meet with them for an open discussion of do's and don'ts. If you are following the guidelines from a handbook they may be out-of-date; Witness rules are ever-changing.

Q. Why do children of Jehovah's Witnesses refuse to salute the flag or stand for the singing of the national anthem?

A. Witnesses believe pledging allegiance to anything other than God is wrong. Jehovah's Witnesses will not pledge or swear allegiance to any government except God's government (Kingdom) which "began to reign" over earth in 1914.

Witnesses teach that by standing for the national anthem or any other patriotic song, one is showing agreement with the song's message. An anthem is a hymn set to music. In the case of patriotic music, one is singing a hymn to a human government rather than to God, idolatry they contend.

It is permissible for a Witness (or child of Witnesses) to stand for the flag salute – but to avoid showing his agreement with the pledge he must not place his hand over his heart, the child must keep his hands at his sides. He may remain standing for the singing of patriotic songs because he is already standing for the flag salute.

The Witness must not stand for the singing of school songs such as "The Alma Mater." Witnesses are not permitted to stand while any prayer is being offered except for prayers by fellow Witnesses. He must not bow his head in agreement or join hands with others, during prayers by non-Witnesses.

Q. Do Jehovah's Witnesses encourage their children to seek a college education?

A. Witnesses were discouraged from furthering their education by attending college. They reason the end of the world's systems are near, so why get caught up in a worldly educational system, a system soon to be destroyed by God?

Additionally, a Witness might be misled by higher education and its criticism of the Bible. One might fall away from "the truth" if exposed to "worldly" philosophy. However, Jehovah's Witnesses are proud of college educated professional people who join their ranks.

Q. How do Jehovah's Witnesses view alcohol and tobacco?

A. Jehovah's Witnesses believe that while alcohol can be consumed in moderation, drunkenness is wrong (see Chapter 5).

Use of tobacco in any form is cause for disfellowshipping. For many years, the Witnesses refused to let smokers serve in a leadership role, but still allowed them in fellowship. Newer revelations showed tobacco to be wrong at all levels. Tobacco users, farmers and sellers are warned and if unrepentant must be disfellowshipped. The Watchtower Society's reason for condemning tobacco use is that tobacco was sometimes used in occult ceremonies. But alcohol has certainly been used as an integral part of pagan ceremonies, likely to a greater extent than tobacco.

Q. Is house-to-house evangelism commanded in the Bible?

A. The foundational verse for Jehovah's Witnesses view on house-to-house preaching is Acts 20:20, "I... have taught you publicly and from house to house."

In 1972 the Watchtower Society recognized that they had misapplied this scripture. Bible commentators generally say that Acts 20:20 uses the expression, "house-to-house," meaning, that is where the church met. So, Paul preached in the houses of believers who had opened their homes as churches. Paul's preaching from house-to-house was in reality preaching from church-to-church.

It was a relief for some Witnesses to know that the difficult house-to-house work was not actually commanded in scripture. Seven years later the Watchtower Society reemphasized the need not to slack off from the house-to-house activity. They instructed that Witnesses, if physically able, should preach house-to-house. Even though the Acts 20:20 verse didn't issue a direct command, house-to-house preaching remains the principal way that Jehovah wanted his work to be conducted, we were told.

Q. How are Jehovah's Witnesses affected by mental illness?

A. Several psychological studies tend to indicate that Jehovah's Witnesses have an abnormally high rate of mental illness. In his extensive report, *"Why Jehovah's Witnesses Have Mental Problems,"* Jerry Bergman, Ph.D. concluded, "A scientific literature review found that the rate of mental illness among Jehovah's Witnesses is considerably above average." Bergman cites seven studies by licensed therapists or psychiatrists. Ranking high on the list of mental illness ailments among Jehovah's Witnesses is paranoia schizophrenia. "Yet they routinely put themselves in the position of encountering opposition when they go door-to-door -- and from this experience often develop paranoia which may explain the fact that paranoia schizophrenia is extremely high among them. A major problem among both leaders and followers is their true believerism causes them to accept conclusions based on ignorance." (Why *Jehovah's Witnesses Have Mental Problems*, Jerry Bergman, Ph.D)

Witness elders are not trained to handle issues of mental illness. Mental health professionals are few or nonexistent among Witnesses.

Q. Why do Kingdom Halls have no windows?

I cannot answer this popular window question authoritatively.

I will speculate.

Buildings without windows are faster and cheaper to construct. While Kingdom halls are financed locally, they are owned by the Watchtower Bible and

Tract Society in Brooklyn, NY. The Society may offer a limited number of building designs to save on architectural fees borne by local Witnesses.

Jehovah Witnesses anticipate persecution. They expect the majority of mankind to turn against them as the world's end approaches. Perhaps the absence of windows in Kingdom Halls is a security measure designed to reduce vandalism from persecutors.

Q. Do Jehovah's Witnesses sing at their meetings?

A. Yes. Singing is usually accompanied by piano. When no piano is available, Witnesses may sing along with recordings from their organization. No solo singing is allowed because that might draw too much attention to the singer, making him or her prideful. The same applies to choirs or small group singing. All singing was congregational.

No Christian hymns are sung at their meetings. Through the years, church hymns were replaced with Witness songs. Witnesses sing about going from house-to-house, of being obedient to Jehovah (whom they believe to be God the Father) and about the paradise earth to come. Few songs have Jesus as their central theme, however Witness songs about Jesus fail to emphasize his Lordship.

As in so many areas of their theology Jehovah's Witnesses have progressively downplayed the preeminence of Christ. This pattern is likewise found in their songs. Watchtower publication, *Revelation Its Grand Climax at Hand*, page 36 states: "In the songbook produced by Jehovah's people in 1905, there were twice as many songs praising Jesus as there were songs praising Jehovah God. In their 1928 songbook, the number of songs extolling Jesus was about the same as the number extolling Jehovah. But in the latest songbook of 1984, Jehovah is honored four times as many songs as is Jesus. ...Love for Jehovah must be <u>preeminent</u>..." (Underlining added for emphasis) However the Bible instructs, "... that in all things he [Jesus] might have the <u>preeminence</u>. For it pleased the Father that in him should all fullness dwell." (see Colossians 1:18, 19, underlining added)

Witness songs are supposedly free of "false" religious influence. Themes like grace, going to heaven or praising Jesus are now absent.

Q. What are the Witness meetings like?

A. Witnesses are expected to attend five meetings each week. On Sundays, the public talk, lasts a little less than an hour. Following the talk is the Watchtower Study. Questions are read from the Watchtower magazine by a conductor. Witnesses "answer" from the material contained in the magazine. Sometimes supporting scripture is read. An assigned reader reads the paragraph just discussed.

If an unknown person in attendance asks a question challenging established beliefs, the meeting's conductor deals with the questioner after the meeting. Only limited discussion is permitted.

Midweek, generally on Tuesday nights, Witnesses attend a book study. Typically lasting an hour, one of the organization's books is discussed and read using the same pattern as the Watchtower Study.

On Thursday nights Witnesses attend the Theocratic Ministry School. The program is college level instruction in speech preparation and delivery. Following the Ministry School is the Service Meeting. Here adherents practice witnessing methods for house-to-house preaching. On Saturday mornings, Witnesses usually spend two hours knocking on doors with the Watchtower and Awake! magazines.

In addition to Sunday meetings, Witnesses meet on Sunday for "sermon work," spending another two hours going house-to-house, explaining their Watchtower gospel to those who might listen.

Circuit Assemblies are held twice each year, with several congregations meeting together and with perhaps 500 to 5,000 attending. Assembly time is spent fellowshipping with Witnesses from other congregations. Methods of door-to-door witnessing are usually demonstrated.

District Assemblies are held annually. Attendance may range from perhaps 5,000 to 10,000. New books and booklets are released for use at local congregation book studies. The new literature will then be offered door-to-door. "New truths" are revealed at District Assemblies. The speakers are mainly from the Brooklyn headquarters. Bible stories are dramatized and attendees are urged to faithfully carry on because Armageddon is near at hand.

In years past much larger conventions were held. For example, in 1958 Witnesses simultaneously filled Yankee Stadium, the Polo Grounds (former NY Giants [baseball] home stadium) and acres of overflow-seating in parking lots; over 253,000 attended. Each attendee is carefully counted, Witnesses are always proud of their numbers. Over 7,000 were baptized at that convention.

Q. When someone criticizes Jehovah's Witnesses isn't that the same as persecution?

A. When a religious group elevates their leaders to an extraordinarily high level, in the case of the Jehovah's Witnesses, looking to their leadership as God's only dispenser of truth on earth, then to question that leadership will be offensive to their followers. It's almost like questioning God himself. Paranoid religious groups cry "persecution" even to the most objective critique of their leaders. Persecution, however, is generally associated with harassment of some kind.

For being a Jehovah's Witness, I was persecuted physically and verbally. Sometimes I was harassed for waking up late sleepers on Sunday mornings, knocking on their doors. Other times I was persecuted for my Witness views on the flag salute, military service, refusing blood transfusions and a host of other issues.

Never was I, as a Jehovah's Witness, ever persecuted for the name of Christ, nor have I ever heard of any Witnesses anywhere who were persecuted for the name of Jesus. Only after leaving the Witnesses and taking a stand as a believer in the Lord Jesus, have I been "insulted because of the name of Christ..." (see 1 Peter 4:14).

As Witness elders informed me at my disfellowshipping hearing, unless I were to repent and stop referring to Jesus as my Lord and my God, I would be cast out of the congregation. My "guilty" conduct, which they considered "unbecoming a Christian," echoed the same confession that Thomas the Apostle made (John 20:28). And additionally, I informed the elders that I, now like Christ's disciples, worshipped Jesus. Nothing could be more abominable to Jehovah's Witnesses.

As a follower of Christ, I loved and worshipped him. "Then they [disciples] worshipped him [Jesus] and returned to Jerusalem with great joy," (Luke 24:52]. Following Watchtower Society guidelines, the elders were obliged to disfellowship me, thus protecting unsuspecting Jehovah's Witnesses from being "corrupted" by my "false" view of Jesus.

Q. Do you have anything positive to say about growing up as a Jehovah's Witness?

A. I am thankful to have been encouraged to read the Bible. This allowed me to learn many verses while my mind was young. The Witnesses have a respect for the Bible (particularly their translation) as the Word of God. Unfortunately, my real authority proved to be the Society's leaders while at the same time I was deceived into believing I was following the Bible.

I am grateful for my moral upbringing. My family's heritage of morality, coupled with the rules of Jehovah's Witnesses, spared me a great deal of heartache. I am thankful to have had two parents who cared a lot about me and loved me, and sought their best for me.

I am grateful cigarettes were forbidden. I am thankful I did not grow up around foul language at home (Mom used to wash my mouth out with soap when I repeated words from the school bus). I am glad I was warned against the sins of the flesh.

I was taught that my future life was dependent upon obedience in religious and secular matters. For example, I believed that if I was killed while disobeying the law (i.e., driving faster than the speed limit) Jehovah would probably not resurrect me but rather leave me in the grave. If I had viewed traffic laws frivolously and received numerous traffic tickets, I would be disfellowshipped. I had plenty of incentive to be law-abiding.

Through Old Testament Law, God showed ancient Israel the impossibility of living a righteous life; that Law pointed to One who could, by grace, save them from sin. In some ways I am grateful that I was under the Watchtower "Law" always feeling guilty and wondering if I was doing wrong. When at last I turned to Jesus, His grace appeared unspeakably precious. The contrast of works versus grace has made me eternally grateful to my Lord, Jesus Christ. As a Jehovah's Witness I was trying to be righteous, that was impossible, but by faith in the saving power of Jesus I was declared righteous the moment I first believed (see Romans 3:20-24).

Q. Do you think disfellowshipping (excommunication) is ever valid?

A. Yes, the concept of breaking fellowship with an unrepentant evildoer is taught in the Bible (see Matthew 18:15-18; 1 Corinthians 5:1-12). Any civic or government organization may expel a member who is a thief or murderer.

Religious organizations represent holy values. A person who insists on continuing his bad behavior, with no intention of changing, rightly needs to be expelled. The Bible instructs specific steps to be taken to restore the errant member. The person giving correction is admonished to do so with a humble spirit – who knows he may be the next to "fall" (see Galatians 6:1- 3).

As a Jehovah's Witness elder, I tried to restore wayward Witnesses. Sometimes they repented and changed behavior. Other times they insisted on ignoring my attempts to help them change their lifestyle. Some we disfellowshipped for unbecoming conduct. Other Witnesses we disfellowshipped for confessing Christ.

My wife and I were disfellowshipped for unashamedly confessing Christ as Lord and God (see John 20:28).

Being cast out of a religious society for confessing Christ is not unique to Jehovah's Witnesses. In the Bible account of the blind man, whom Jesus sent to the pool of Siloam for healing, the man's parents dared not reveal who healed their son – "… they were afraid of the Jews, for already the Jews had decided that anyone who acknowledged that Jesus was the Christ would be put out of the synagogue," (John 9:22).

Disfellowshipping can be used correctly as a last step in discipline, or it can be abused, expelling the very ones whom God may be raising up to bring reform to a fallible organization.

Q. Should Christians compliment Jehovah's Witnesses?

A. Jesus never complimented false teachers. "Woe to you, teachers of the law and Pharisees, you hypocrites! You travel over land and sea to win a single convert, and when he becomes one, you make him twice as much a son of hell as yourself" (Matthew 23:15).

Sometimes Christian householders would complement me, "If we Christians had the zeal you Jehovah's Witnesses have, we could win the world for Christ." I never accepted those words graciously. I would think, "Then why aren't you out doing house-to-house witnessing like God commanded?" As I departed the sincere householder I was even more determined to expose "false religion." "I am actually doing what God commanded," I thought – "If that householder had the truth they would be out working for God like me." The most-quoted-of-all scripture by Jehovah's Witnesses would come to mind, "Faith without works is dead."

Q. Should I discuss doctrine with Jehovah's Witnesses?

A. Paul wrote, "The man without the Spirit does not accept the things that come from the Spirit of God, for they are foolishness to him, and he cannot understand them, because they are spiritually discerned" (1 Corinthians 2:14).

Evangelist Vance Havner once said that trying to explain spiritual things to an unsaved person is like trying to describe a sunset to a blind man. Jehovah's Witnesses believe that only their "spirit anointed ones" can understand the things of God; the remaining Witnesses (8 million) must depend on these special ones to explain the Bible. They believe the Bible was not written for the average Jehovah's Witness, but rather it was written directly to those anointed ones (totaling 144,000 over 2,000 years, today with about 10,000 still on earth).

I believe if a Christian talks doctrine with Jehovah's Witnesses he may convey the false notion that they are fellow Christians. "... for they are foolishness to him, and he cannot understand them, because they are spiritually discerned" (see above quote).

Paul declared what everyone needs to hear. "When I came to you, brothers, I did not come with eloquence or superior wisdom as I proclaimed to you the testimony about God. For I resolved to know nothing while I was with you except Jesus Christ and Him crucified" (1 Corinthians 2:1,2).

I am convinced that Jehovah's Witnesses, as everyone else without Christ, need to hear about "Jesus Christ and Him crucified." They, as I did, need to hear that someone loved them so much that he was willing to die for them, saving them from their sins. "For God so loved the world that He gave his one and only Son, that whoever believes in Him shall not perish but have eternal life" (John 3:16).

Furthermore, as a Jehovah's Witness I rarely engaged in an honest debate with anyone. I had a plethora of diversionary remarks intended to derail objections and leave the questioner in a state of confusion. An example:

Householder: "You people don't believe in hell."

Me: "Would you hold your disobedient child's hand on a hot stove to punish him? How could a loving God ever punish his children by sending them to a fiery hell?"

Householder: "But Jesus taught a literal hell in Luke 16 when he spoke of the rich man and Lazarus."

Me: "Don't you realize that the story of Lazarus and the rich man is not literal but only a parable?"

I would keep presenting diversionary comments until the householder became confused or simply gave up. Of course, I could not adequately explain away Jesus' many references to hell.

A well-prepared householder might have a list of scriptures proving hell. Even if they could have overwhelmed me with proof texts and convinced me of the reality of hell through scripture, my real need centered not on the understanding or accepting doctrine. My real need centered on my lostness and my need to believe that there is a loving Savior waiting to receive me as His child, forgiving all my sins.

Another popular evasive tactic used by Witnesses when confronted about the way they have mistreated their own people is to respond, "We're not like that anymore, we have changed a lot." Once again, the real issue is sidestepped, an honest discussion is avoided.

Sometimes Christians will tell me with great pride how they stumped Jehovah's Witnesses. "The Witnesses just didn't know how to answer me," they relate. "They just turned around and walked away!" I always feel badly when I hear those remarks. How much better to lovingly ask the Witnesses about their need for forgiveness of sins, offering to tell them one's own experience of trusting Christ as Savior.

Q. Does the Bible forbid inviting Jehovah's Witnesses into my house?

A. The scripture reference in question is 2 John 1:10,11. "If anyone comes to you and does not bring this teaching, do not take him into your house or welcome him. Anyone who welcomes him shares in his wicked works." John the Apostle is warning a Christian woman who evidently has an assembly of Christians meeting in her house. He advises her not to let a false teacher into her house (church).

Some scholars have interpreted this verse to mean any believer's house. Other scholars believe it means not to let a false teacher speak in the local church, because at that time Christians met in homes.

A person has control over their own home, I suggest inviting any sincere person into your house. I see it as an opportunity to tell that person about my testimony for Jesus Christ. But I would not allow anyone to teach false doctrines in my house.

I do not think we have to make deals with Jehovah's Witnesses, as in, "I'll listen as you tell your story for 30 minutes and then you must agree to listen as I tell my story for 30 minutes."

Always attempt to share your knowledge of Christ with Jehovah's Witnesses. Please do not tell them, "I just read a book by an ex-Jehovah's Witness, he tells how terribly wrong you are." That is an easy way to dismiss Witnesses, but it leaves them with no evidence of your faith in Christ.

On occasion, people would post a sign on their door reading, "NO JW s or LDS." Imagine seeing a sign at a Christian home, "Welcome, JW s and LDS, please let me share my Jesus story with you."

Q. Why must Jehovah's Witnesses refuse to take my church literature?

A. The Watchtower organization forbids it; Witnesses are only allowed to read religious literature published by the Watchtower Society.

Q. How could you have been so deceived to have believed all those things taught by Jehovah's Witnesses?

A. When religious teachings are sincerely instilled in you from childhood, there is strong reason to believe that your mother and father are telling the truth.

All people should question their religious authorities if they have any doubt about doctrine or church practice. "Now the Bereans were of more noble character than the Thessalonians, for they received the message with great eagerness and examined the Scriptures every day to see if what Paul said was true" (Acts 17:11).

Q. Briefly, what is the primary distinction between Jehovah's Witnesses and biblical Christianity?

A. The "Jesus" of Jehovah's Witnesses was created by God; he is not the Creator of all things. The Jesus of the Bible is Creator of everything (see John 1:3; Colossians 1:16).

The Watchtower "Jesus" is not God, but rather "a god." The Bible rejects this notion, teaching that God made no other "gods" (see Isaiah 43: 10 b). But Jehovah's Witnesses nonetheless teach that there exists a greater God (Jehovah) and a lesser god (Jesus).

Because the Witness "Jesus" is not God, his sacrificial death could not fully pay for the sins of those who believe; he is only a partial savior. Therefore, in order to gain everlasting life Witnesses must try to pay what their "Jesus" could not pay. They attempt this by adding their own good works as a requirement for salvation. Because they think that they must participate in their salvation, they necessarily become co-saviors. As co-saviors they unknowingly exalt themselves to godlike status in order to be saved from their sins and inherit everlasting life. But any attempt at self-salvation is idolatry (See pg. 163).

Therefore, Jehovah's Witnesses cannot know God's forgiveness now, but if they continue faithful in good works, they believe, they might be reconciled to God and finally have their sins forgiven. This reconciliation follows God's final test of mankind's obedience, at least 1000 years from now. Of course, without faith in the true Savior, the Jesus of the Bible, there can be no hope for eternal life (see Acts 4:12)

Jehovah's Witnesses are not just another Christian sect or denomination; their refusal to acknowledge that Jesus is Lord and God (see John 21:28) has placed them outside the realm of Christianity.

Watchtower Shunning - Is it Hate-speech?

I believe Jehovah's Witnesses push their shunning to the extreme, having exceeded all biblical guidelines of church discipline. I find nothing remotely Christian in Watchtower shunning.

A turning point in their doctrine of shunning may have been when they introduced the destructive word "hate" into their diatribe against disfellowshipped members. Speaking of such ex-Jehovah's Witnesses, note what the June 15, 1980 Watchtower magazine announced, "More than that, we want to *hate* those who willingly show themselves *haters* of Jehovah, *haters* of what is good...we *hate*, not in the sense of wanting to do harm...but in the sense of avoiding them as we would *poison* or a *poisonous* snake, for they can *poison* us spiritually." (Italics added)

Compare the Watchtower's harsh words with those of the Lord Jesus: "But I tell you, love your enemies and pray for those who persecute you, that you may be children of your Father in Heaven. He causes His sun to rise on the evil and the good, and sends rain on the righteous and the unrighteous."

Particularly disturbing, are reports I've personally heard: A child states, "I don't want to love you Mommy because if I do, I will die with you when Jehovah destroys you in Armageddon. Just come back to the meetings and get reinstated and then we can be together, forever."

Or a child screaming, "I hate you mommy! You Apostate! Bitch! You're disfellowshipped, Jehovah is going to destroy you in Armageddon!"

Even more disheartening and abusive, a child physically throwing his shunned mother to the ground, injuring her frail body. Meanwhile, the Jehovah's Witness parent stands applauding the child's conduct.

Can it be *proven* that the horrible fruitage I have just described resulted from the Watchtower's warnings "to hate those" who have been disfellowshipped? I don't believe so, however, I do believe that history demonstrates that preaching hate, rather than Christ's doctrine of love, ultimately leads to violence.

The violence may begin as spiritual violence, as in "Unless you return to the Watchtower Society, Jehovah will destroy you, you will be annihilated forever!" I've sometimes witnessed a 'hatred of God' attitude among ex-Jehovah's Witnesses, they just couldn't seem to ever please the demanding Watchtower god.

Add to such a pronouncement this warning, "You know what will happen, you will lose your Jehovah's Witness friends and family!" Another lever of fear is instilled into those shunned. Finally, Watchtower warnings to "hate" those who are shunned may lead to physical violence as described in the before mentioned testimony.

The Watchtower tirade, against those shunned, keeps mounting. Will it continue until there are lawsuits accusing Jehovah's Witnesses of inciting violence against disfellowshipped members? *Watchtower* 1993 Oct 1 pg. 19 continues, "...when the bad becomes so ingrained that it is an inseparable part of their (ex-Jehovah's Witnesses) makeup, then a Christian (meaning Jehovah's Witness) must hate (in the biblical sense of the word) those who have inseparably attached themselves to badness, (particularly those who turn from the Watchtower Society to follow historic Christianity), ...they feel a loathing toward those who have made themselves God's enemies." (parenthesis to include my thoughts)

Back to the Bible, once again, "If your enemy is hungry, feed him; if he is thirsty, give him something to drink. In doing this, you will heap burning coals on his head. Do not be overcome with evil, but overcome evil with good." Romans 12:20-21

The 'loathing' toward the disfellowshipped person seems to be escalating, with increasingly strict warnings to cut off all ties with those being shunned. Associating with such disfellowshipped ones will result in the offending Jehovah's Witness, though in good standing, also being cast out; therefore, spiritually dead and also subject to everlasting annihilation. Not only do admonitions appear in print, but they are portrayed on digital media available to congregations and conventions (and now on the internet, for the entire world to observe). Warnings advise against responding to a shunned person's emails; or other electronic communications including refusing to answer a phone call when the caller ID identifies an incoming call from a disfellowshipped child.

A story shared with me from an ex-Jehovah's Witness tells of a daughter whose mother (a practicing Jehovah's Witness) will be attending a Jehovah's Witness conference where she will share before hundreds how she is proving her integrity to Jehovah by totally shunning her 'apostate' daughter (now a born-again follower of Jesus). This sharing will take place in front of the daughter's children. So, goes the negative speech. Is all this hate speech? I think the following article will help you decide.

Isabella Botticelli writes, "Snakes, contaminated soil, liars, mentally diseased, part of the Antichrist…" These are just a few of the words heard at the 2013 Watchtower district convention.

"The frightening hate speech above describes the nature of an 'apostate', an example of loaded language used to strike terror into the heart of Jehovah's Witnesses. Peppered throughout the talk entitled, 'Beware of Human Apostates', speakers used additional negative labels, and urged their followers to avoid them lest they end up in the dystopian hell-scape occupied by apostates. Although the talk outlined three ways to identify a 'true apostate', the organization fosters and encourages its followers to include all dissenters from their religion as apostates. These include all who have been disfellowshipped (excommunicated) from the religion, even minors.

"While Jehovah's Witnesses, in general, are used to hearing their leaders criticize ex-members and people of other religions, with this year's world-wide conventions, the intensity of this hate speech directed towards non-Witnesses is increasing. Unfortunately, there is little to be done about such speech in the United States. Unless, you are directly inciting violence, hateful words are protected by the First Amendment. However, some Western European countries, having been victims of horrifying hate speech that did incite violence during WWII, have laws to protect citizens against hate speech.

"This summer, in the convention cities of Silkeborg and Herlumagle in Denmark, some ex-members were appalled as they listened to Watchtower leaders describe them as snakes, a deadly virus, and other loathsome analogies. A Danish support group for ex-Jehovah's Witnesses pressed charges against the

Watchtower for violating article 266b of the Danish Criminal Code. The code, in part states:

> *"(1) Any person who publicly or with the intention of dissemination to a wide circle of people makes a statement or imparts other information threatening, insulting or degrading a group of persons on account of their race, colour, national or ethnic, belief or sexual orientation shall be liable to a fine, simple detention or imprisonment for a term not exceeding two years."*

"The head of the Documentation and Advisory Centre on Racial Discrimination, Niels Hansen agreed that the Watchtower has exceeded the bounds of Danish free speech laws. As reported in the July 25, 2013 issue of *Kristeligt Dagblad*, Hansen stated, 'The speeches are the same type of Rhetoric that we heard against the Jews in Europe in the 1930's. This is precisely what the anti-discrimination article was introduced to restrain.' Currently, police are reviewing the case; it will likely be several weeks before any action is taken. As a direct result of the complaint filed against Jehovah's Witnesses, the newspaper, *Berlingske Nyhedsbureau*, dated July 30, 2013, reported that several political organizations are now recommending that religious groups be monitored more closely to be sure they are compliant with Danish regulations ("Society is Ready to be Looked [at] on the cards").

"This is not the first time Jehovah's Witnesses have been to court in Denmark. In 2006, the religion was literally blasted out of the court for trying to sue Danish newspaper *Ekstra Bladet* for slander (libel). Three articles revealing the sever pedophile problem within the organization were not appreciated by the Danish Jehovah's Witnesses Branch Office Executive Committee. Watchtower requested over $62,000 in damages when the paper criticized their child abuse reporting policies, and for revealing over 23,000 cases of child abuse being hidden by the organization's headquarters in Brooklyn, New York. According to *Ekstra Bladet* on December 6, 2006. Watchtower spokesperson Erik Jorgensen was forced to admit that they routinely hide pedophiles, while simultaneously expelling member for minor infractions, stating that, "...convicted pedophiles can continue as members of both the congregations and their family." Judge Stkholm found all the articles to be newsworthy and an "important public matter as well as a legal criticism of the sect." Watchtower was sentenced to pay almost $9,000 in legal fees.

"Watchtower is brazening in going after others to repress their right of free speech, but it is perfectly acceptable for them to use malevolent hate speech to criticize ex-members, other Religious organizations, governments, and the world in general. Let's not forget their own hypocritical words in the June 22, 2000 issue of *Awake!* aptly entitled 'Propaganda Can Be Deadly':

'Some people insult those who disagree with them by questioning character or motives instead of focusing on the facts. Name calling slaps a negative, easy to remember label onto a person, group or idea. The name caller hopes that the label will stick. If people reject the person or the idea on the basis of the negative label instead of weighing the evidence for themselves, the name caller's strategy has worked.'

"Evidently, it does not bother Watchtower to do the opposite of what they preach. This hypocrisy has not gone unnoticed by other organizations. Marci Hamilton, author and Chair in Public Law at Benjamin N. Cardozo School of Law, Yeshiva University, had this to say:

"The Jehovah's Witnesses religious organization is rightly credited with establishing important free speech precedent in the United States...It is extraordinarily ironic, then, that the Jehovah's Witnesses have recently, in Denmark, taken the position that speech, including speech by the press should be punished and suppressed. It appears that when the topic is alleged clergy abuse within the organization, its position on freedom speech makes a 180-degree turn. Apparently, the Jchovah's Witnesses support free speech for themselves, but not for their critics.

"With the Watchtower cruelly labeling ex-members as 'apostates', and blackmailing those inside to crush ties by shunning them, it is becoming easier to unmask the damage they are causing by their escalating hate speech and fear mongering. Whatever the outcome in Denmark, AAWA (Advocates for Awareness of Watchtower Abuse) will continue to take an organized lead against exposing the Watchtower for their dangerous practices that harm millions."

So, what do you think? Are Jehovah's Witnesses guilty of using hate speech to shame those leaving their religion? Are they using harsh, un-Christlike words to intimidate any who might dare even minimal contact with the shunned family and friends?

Botticelli, Isabella. Watchtower Hate Speech Leads to Legal Troubles in Denmark

AAWA.co, Vol. Issue 3. 2013. Web. 5 April 2017

AAWA.co>co>uploads>2013/6>N...

What About the Pedophilia Epidemic Among Jehovah's Witnesses?

This book, Banished from Jehovah's Witnesses, is on display at a small gallery where I work part time. The most common remark I've heard: "Oh, I didn't know Jehovah's Witnesses were not Christians." However a gentleman, while recently eying my book display, surprised with me with his comment, "Jehovah's Witnesses, I hear they are having legal troubles over their failure to report pedophiles."

The man was speaking sincerely, with no sign of religious prejudice. He was simply commenting on what he had heard. I was surprised to learn that the JW pedophilia issue was moving into public view.

Only recently had I learned of the seriousness of the situation from both an ex-JW who claimed she was personally violated and then my follow up research revealed a multitude of accusations.

These accusations center around the alleged victim not being able to provide an additional eyewitness to the JW elders. The case might then be handled by the elders requesting that the minor child meet face-to-face with her accuser. Already shamed, the victim may think she (he) is somehow responsible for the sexual abuse. The perpetrator denies all allegations and the victim may be rebuked by the elders for bringing an accusation without two or more witnesses to the sin. The child returns to her former situation only to be sexually abused again.

During my years in JW leadership I recall a case. A new family moved into our small congregation. We were overjoyed to have them (father, mother, and 15-year-old daughter) join with us. The man, whom I'll call "John" was friendly and helpful, always assisting people in need and eager to serve in our congregation. Our leadership recommended that he be appointed as a ministerial servant [similar to deacon]. The congregation from which John and his family had moved, requested that our committee meet with them. The other committee recommended that we not use John as a 'servant' in our congregation because of an accusation against him. They read a letter written by John's step-daughter, a minor child. It included graphic details of being raped by step-dad, John. When confronted, John denied. Since that committee had only one witness to the incident, they told us that they could not determine whether such a sin had taken place or not. From that point forward, we were careful not to use John in leadership positions.

All committee members from both congregations were totally ignorant of how sexual child abuse should be handled. Even though we elders enforced scores of Witness rules within our congregations, I'd never heard of any mandatory reporting laws pertaining to pedophilia. Perhaps they were mentioned at Kingdom Ministry school which I had attended, but I had no recollection of any mention on how to handle such cases involving sexual abuse against children.

In more recent times it may be that Witness elders have reasoned, "We are not 'clergymen.' We, JWs, have unrelentingly exposed Satan's agents, 'the clergy of Christendom,' for being responsibility for nearly all evils in the world, like wars, hatred, moral failure, etc. Since we, JWs, reject the 'Clergy' label; we are therefore not responsible to obey laws which require Clergy to report sexual abuse against children."

It appears that the Watchtower Organization may be spending millions in dealing with this issue. It is likely that most cases will be settled out-of-court offering secret settlements thus sparing the shame of public trial.

Recommended Reading

Books:

Apostles of Denial, Edmond Gruss, "An examination and expose' of the history, doctrines and claims of the Jehovah's Witnesses."

Handbook of Today's Religions, Josh McDowell / Don Stewart, "A reference work written for all concerned Christians who desire to have a more discerning, broader-based knowledge of the major cults and belief systems that diabolically oppose Bible-based Christianity."

The Jehovah's Witnesses' New Testament, Robert H. Countess, Ph.D., "A critical analysis of The New World Translation of The Christian Greek Scriptures." [Jehovah's Witnesses Bible]

The Kingdom of The Cults, (Updated), Walter Martin, Hank Hanegraaff, "Scholarly yet readable and engaging, The Kingdom of The Cults evaluates each cult movement's history and beliefs, showing how each cult's teaching contrast with true biblical theology."

Ministries:

MM Outreach Inc., www.outreachinc.com provides internet pages, books, booklets, DVD's pertaining to cults. See the Pagan Roots of Jehovah's Witnesses.

Watchman Fellowship, Inc., Box 7681, Columbus, GA, 31908. www.watchmanfellowship.org "An independent Christian research and apologetic ministry focusing on new religious movements, cults, the occult and the New Age Movement."

Index

"

"a god" 73, 178
"Amazing Grace" 70, 72, 92, 111

1

144,000 ... 49, 50, 51, 52, 53, 59, 66, 67, 180, 183, 184, 186, 204
1914 .... 21, 22, 25, 26, 27, 175, 193
1925 25
1975 .... 27, 28, 29, 65

A

abusive churches 129
Aletheia Springs 121, 124, 125, 129
Apostasy 55
Armageddon 14, 17, 25, 26, 27, 28, 29, 34, 38, 57, 116, 153, 155, 162, 175, 190, 199, 210
Athanasius 159, 161
Augustine 154

B

Baptism 118, 120, 142

C

Cana 42, 47, 48, 55
Catholic 65, 104, 114, 142
Christmas 5, 6, 7, 8, 21, 34, 58, 59, 82, 85, 86, 94, 101, 144, 190, 192
City of God 154
Crisis of Conscience 129

D

Da Vinci Code 159
Death 13
Disfellowshipping 99, 203

F

Franklin Heights Baptist Church 125
Franklinville 51, 71

H

Hell 146, 150, 154
Holidays 190
Holy Spirit 17, 18, 79, 84, 118, 122, 123, 124, 141, 151, 167, 169, 176, 177, 178, 182, 183, 184, 193

I

In Search of Christian Freedom 129
Israel 2, 9, 30, 33, 42, 61, 68, 90, 95, 117, 118, 119, 122, 126, 127, 130, 131, 137, 155, 173, 182, 202

J

Jerry Stiles 121, 124
Jerusalem ...... i, 11, 19, 55, 70, 76, 78, 87, 94, 96, 102, 157, 158, 166, 168, 201
Jewish people 30, 121
Judicial Committee 56, 57, 59, 60, 83

K

Kennedy 24
Kingdom Hall. 15, 16, 18, 49, 60, 61, 64, 78, 81, 83, 84, 85, 93, 97, 131, 185
Kingdom Ministry School 47

L

Lord .... i, viii, 19, 20, 22, 23, 61, 64, 72, 75, 80, 83, 84, 85, 92, 97, 99, 100, 104, 107, 108, 109, 112, 114, 115, 117, 131, 132, 136, 138, 140, 142, 145, 148, 155, 159, 166, 167, 175, 176, 179, 180, 181, 182, 183, 187, 200, 202, 203, 209, 210
Lord Jesus... i, viii, 20, 22, 61, 75, 80, 83, 92, 115, 140, 148, 159, 167, 175, 176, 179, 180, 182, 183, 200, 210
Lord's Prayer 64, 72, 142

M

Megiddo church 158
Michael Jackson 35
Mona Lisa 42

N

Nazareth Village 49, 54
New Light 20, 52
New World Translation ii, 16, 36, 50, 73, 172, 174, 178, 220

P

Palestine 30
Persecution 200
Prince 35
Pyramid 20, 22, 31

R

Resurrection 126
Roman road 55, 61

S

Santa Claus 5, 6
Shepherd 49, 53, 54
Son of God 28, 176, 177

T

Tobacco 194
Trinity ... 56, 67, 76, 79, 83, 91, 98, 109, 123, 124, 151, 159, 160, 161, 177

U

Universalist Church 6, 18

W

Watchman Fellowship 91, 129, 220
Watchtower Farms 45
Watchtower magazine 21, 22, 172, 176, 198, 210
Watchtower Society 6, 9, 14, 16, 17, 20, 21, 23, 25, 26, 27, 28, 30, 39, 43, 52, 57, 60, 64, 65, 71, 86, 91, 93,

99, 101, 105, 108, 113, 129, 149, 159, 174, 175, 179, 186, 189, 195, 201, 208, 211, 212

Western Light Tabernacle 81, 119, 121

WRVL 81

Z

Zionist 30, 173

Zippori 42, 47, 48

Made in the USA
Middletown, DE
14 June 2021